SUN RECORDS

AN ORAL HISTORY

Other titles in the **For the Record** series:

Black Sabbath
Sam and Dave

George Clinton and P-Funk (summer 1998)
Sly and the Family Stone (summer 1998)
The Women of Motown (summer 1998)

SUN RECORDS

AN ORAL HISTORY

by John Floyd

EDITED BY DAVE MARSH

AVON BOOKS NEW YORK

For Charlie Rich and Roy Orbison

AVON BOOKS
A division of
The Hearst Corporation
1350 Avenue of the Americas
New York, New York 10019

Copyright © 1998 by John Floyd
Designed and produced by March Tenth, Inc.
Cover design by Harry Choron
Published by arrangement with March Tenth, Inc.
Visit our website at **http://www.AvonBooks.com**
Library of Congress Catalog Card Number:97-94612
ISBN: 0-380-79373-3

First Avon Books Trade Printing: February 1998

Printed in the U.S.A.

OPM   10 9 8 7 6 5 4 3 2 1

CONTENTS

	Acknowledgments	VII
	Editor's Note	IX
	Introduction: The Great Musical Menagerist	XI
1	Sunrise	1
2	Elvis and the Kings of Western Bop	27
3	Goin' to the Rockhouse	60
4	Dixie Flyer	93
5	706 Union Avenue	114
6	Sunset	143
	Discography	156
	Bibliography	182
	Index	185

ACKNOWLEDGMENTS

A lot of people helped me out while I was working on this book, through guidance, support, and putting me in touch with the right people. For contacts, phone numbers, and directional tips, thanks go out to John Stivers, Reggie Churchwell, Ron Hall, Sue Whitall, Maggie and Alton Warwick, Steve Satterwhite, Kevin Roe, David Cantwell, Lance Cowan, Judy Peiser, Billy Miller, Leslie Ann Myers, Henry Gross, and Garry Talent.

I owe a mess of gratitude to Dave Marsh and Sandra Choron for giving me the chance to participate in the series. Christine Tague lent her extraordinary copy-editing skills to the manuscript and made many astute suggestions and recommendations. My friend Tom Graves—who gave me my first full-time writing gig many years ago—graciously allowed me to use his unpublished interview with Rufus Thomas. Eddie Hankins fielded numerous calls from me in search of names, dates, and records; read through many of the interview transcripts; and listened to me rant and rave about all manner of Sun-related trivia. His friendship and assistance were invaluable to the completion of this book. Harry Choron turned it all into a book.

My parents, Margie and Carlyle Floyd, provided my first exposure to the magic and mystery of Sun Records through their countless spinnings of albums and singles by Elvis, Johnny Cash, Charlie Rich, and Jerry Lee Lewis. On warm Saturday and Sunday afternoons I would hear "Folsom Prison Blues," "Good Rockin' Tonight," "Great Balls of Fire," "Lonely Weekends," and countless other Sun classics drift from the open windows of our North Memphis home as I helped my dad scrub down the cars out in the driveway. I don't think either of them will ever know the impact those weekend sessions had on my young, impressionable mind.

Nor will Billy Lee Riley ever know just how thrilling it was for me to sit with him at Sun and listen to him spin tales—pointing from the control room into the studio, showing me exactly where he was standing when he added that song-closing guitar strum on Jerry Lee Lewis's "Crazy Arms," tracing the path of his legendary drunken rampage at Sun in 1958. As for Roland Janes, what can I say? He put up with more phone calls and pestering than anyone deserves, and I can't thank him enough for his participation in this book. I hope he doesn't regret it.

Among those always on hand with kind, encouraging words: Roger Moneymaker, Richard Martin, Kurt Dietz, Reva Morphew, Paul Christie, Sarah Kingsbury, Marcus Hartsfield, Martina Moore, Dunstan Prial, Teddy Allen, Rhett Biletti, Ralph Stewart, Sherman Willmott, and Andria Lisle. Special thanks is owed to Tim Sampson, Sandra Jackson Hall, Hal Norville, and Leonard Gill for always making Memphis home no matter how far I roam.

Finally, words cannot do justice in describing the love, support, and motivational prodding I've received from Judy Cantor. She held the light in my darkest hours, pushed me back to the computer when fatigue sent me wandering, and was always there with a comforting, "Don't worry, babe. It'll get done." As usual, she was right.

EDITOR'S NOTE

For the Record is a series of books that presents performers from the history of rock and soul music—from rockabilly to funk, from R&B to post-punk—in their own words. *For the Record* isn't concerned with the most obvious stars; exploring the stories untold and half-told which need to be properly retold constitutes our mission.

While our authors and editors shape the series by their choice of subjects for the books and the topics discussed within them, one of the things we have learned early on is that the true direction of the volumes will be provided by their speakers. Thus the books that make up *For the Record* will not always talk about what other books on the same subject talk about—if an artist isn't especially interested in what happens in the recording studio but has a fascination with what happens in hotel rooms after live gigs, that's what you'll get. So while we try to cover all the bases, sometimes we learn that what we thought was home plate isn't even on the playing field.

But surprises are what good books are all about. We guarantee this much: Each of our subjects has a story to tell, and here, each of them tells it, in words as close to their own as we can manage it. Each, we believe, casts a unique spotlight.

—Dave Marsh

INTRODUCTION

The Great Musical Menagerist

Although it is rightly celebrated as the place where blues, pop, and country met as one and became rock and roll, there's something greater that connects the music recorded at Sun Studio by Sam Phillips—something that goes far beyond anything as simple as the blues swing in this country tune or the honky-tonk snap in that R&B wailer. You can hear it in Howlin' Wolf's "My Baby Walked Off" and Elvis Presley's "Good Rockin' Tonight," in Pat Hare's "I'm Gonna Murder My Baby" and Charlie Rich's "Lonely Weekends," in Jerry Lee Lewis's "Whole Lotta Shakin' Goin' On" and James Cotton's "Cotton Crop Blues." What you hear is a moment when the singers and musicians looked deep into their lives and emotions, found a part of their soul that maybe they didn't even know existed, and projected it into Phillips's tape machine. Sometimes it was enhanced with a bit of tape-delay echo, or maybe a micro-

SUN
RECORD COMPANY
Memphis Music
U-89 BMI
Blues Vocal
2:20
MYSTERY TRAIN
(Parker)
LITTLE JUNIOR'S
BLUE FLAMES
192
MEMPHIS, TENNESSEE

phone was placed in *just the right spot* to add an ethereal ambiance to the proceedings. But the soul was there, frozen in time but alive for the ages. Those songs, and many others just as good, bristle with the sound of discovery, of potential suddenly turning into perfection.

Moments like that were almost routine at Sun, and over a period of about ten years Phillips and his eclectic and ever-changing stable of artists created the foundation on which most modern blues and nearly all rock and roll firmly rests. The label's achievements have been amply documented in books, album liner notes, and countless magazine articles, but they remain no less staggering nearly fifty years after Phillips—a native of Alabama born January 5, 1923—started the Memphis Recording Service in a small, narrow storefront on Union Avenue.

Phillips was already an established radio man when he opened the studio, having produced and hosted shows in Muscle Shoals, Decatur, and Nashville before moving to Memphis in 1945. There, he first took a job as an announcer at WREC, where his older brother Jud Phillips sang in the mornings as part of the Jollyboys Quartet. In 1949, in need of extra cash to support his growing family, Phillips got the idea to open a studio to record, as the slogan went, "Anything–Anywhere–Anytime." Mostly that meant weddings, bar mitzvahs, speeches, and commercials, but Phillips was also able to record the local bluesmen he had been infatuated with since the late thirties, when he first encountered Beale Street en route to Dallas with some church friends from Alabama.

Although he has said that he never had a desire to start a record company, Phillips almost immediately entered into a partnership with Memphis disc jockey Dewey Phillips, related in spirit if not blood, to do just that. The label, christened Phillips, issued its one and only record in the summer of 1950: Joe Hill Louis's "Gotta Let You Go"/"Boogie in the Park," a raucous pairing by a local one-man band. Only three hundred copies were pressed; the poorly distributed disc promptly sank with hardly a trace. Phillips's work with Louis did lead, however, to a partnership of sorts with the Bihari brothers—Joe, Saul, and Jules—who headed the Los Angeles-based Modern label and were about to start up a subsidiary imprint, RPM. Phillips would record local talent in his studio and ship the results to the Biharis for release. (He also worked up a similar deal with Leonard Chess in Chicago, much to the chagrin of the Bihari clan.)

Even before he introduced the Sun label in 1952, Phillips had already recorded some of the most important blues artists, most notably B. B. King and Howlin' Wolf, as well as some of R&B's biggest early hits, including Jackie Brenston's "Rocket 88." Once Sun made its proper debut with "Driving Slow," a moody instrumental by Memphis saxman Johnny London, Phillips's studio became a magnet for blues and R&B performers throughout the mid-South, attracting everyone from Junior Parker and Bobby "Blue" Bland to Rufus Thomas and Little Milton, all of whom would become influential and popular in the 1960s.

From there the story of Sun reads less like history and more like a combination of fable and myth. Always on the lookout for a white man who could sing with the soul and feel of a black man, Phillips (or, depending upon whom you believe, Phillips's assistant, Marion Keisker) found him in 1954—a shy but sharp-dressed nineteen-year-old named Elvis Presley. Together Phillips and his young artist created rock and roll and brought Sun to the forefront of a pop music revolution with a battalion that counted in its ranks Carl Perkins, Jerry Lee Lewis, Roy Orbison, Charlie Rich, and a host of other worthy soldiers.

The Sun Records story is ultimately the Sam Phillips story— one based on his determination to lend voice and a little dignity to the unheard masses of poor Southerners who entered his studio. There is a tendency, however, to gloss over some of Phillips's shortcomings as a producer and a record man (just as there is a tendency to overlook the contributions of Phillips's assistants, most notably Jack Clement and Roland Janes). Chief among those shortcomings was Phillips's inability to harness the talents of the wildly gifted Roy Orbison and Charlie Rich, who had to leave the label in order to make their best records. As for Sun's notoriously low royalty payments, they may have been no worse than those of other labels at the time, but that doesn't mean a lot of people didn't get paid—or, at least, didn't get paid what they deserved. And because Phillips proved incapable of carrying Sun's legacy into the 1960s (he spent the decade instead buying radio stations and investing in the Holiday Inn chain), the Sun story feels unfinished, despite the 1969 sale to Shelby Singleton that provides its final chapter.

In the long run, though, little of that matters, and if you're going to cut someone some slack, Sam Phillips better be at the top of the list. Not that he needs it: The man did more to alter the direction of popular music than anyone this side of Louis Armstrong, from the litany of artists he thrust upon the staid pop scene of the 1950s to his numerous innovations in the studio, which helped to turn the recording process from one that simply documented the sound of a live band to one in which the studio and the men running the equipment were integral components of the music. At Sun they had to be. After all, they were recording souls.

ONE

Sunrise

More than forty years after the fact, it's hard to grasp exactly how important Sam Phillips's role is in the pantheon of American music history. Even if he'd never issued a record on the shining yellow Sun label, even if Elvis Presley had never entered his small recording studio on the outskirts of downtown Memphis at 706 Union Avenue, Phillips would rank as one of the most visionary record producers of our time on the basis of his early fifties blues work.

Take a look at the roster of blues artists who made their debuts at the Memphis Recording Service—opened by Phillips at the dawn of 1950 and rechristened Sun two years later—and you get a sense of the man's impact: Howlin' Wolf, a gravel-voiced acolyte of Delta blues pioneer Charley Patton, whose music once prompted Phillips to pronounce, "This is for me. This is where the soul of man never dies"; Junior Parker, whose tight, propulsive combo found a perfect balance between rural boogie and uptown blues, whose handful of Sun singles provided a partial blueprint for rockabilly and, therefore, rock and roll; B. B. King, whose impassioned vocals and biting guitar work would make him the single most influential bluesman of the postwar era; harmonica aces Walter

Horton and James Cotton, who would each help Muddy Waters navigate two of his greatest Chicago groups; Joe Hill Louis and Doctor Ross, one-man-bands who could level city blocks with their blazing, over-amped raunch. And don't forget Rosco Gordon, Rufus Thomas, Little Milton, and Earl Hooker. These men stood at the forefront of the blues. They tower over its past and present, their innovations still providing the benchmark against which every artist after them must ultimately be measured.

By the time Phillips opened the Memphis Recording Service, the blues was in what today seems like a period of transition: It had long since emerged from its Delta roots but had barely begun the journey north. Which is to say it was evolving from an acoustic-based music into something electric, with a louder rhythmic drive with more power behind it. Which is also to say that the blues sides Phillips recorded in Memphis shatter one of the great myths in the blues—that it became a truly electric music only after its migration to urban-industrial meccas such as Chicago and Detroit. Without taking a revisionist shot at the legacies of Muddy Waters, Little Walter Jacobs, or Howlin' Wolf's post-Memphis output, it's safe to say that the blues has never sounded as mean, raw, or intense as it did on countless days and nights at 706 Union Avenue. Amplifiers were cranked way past the point of distortion, guitars slashed like straight razors, rickety drum kits were pounded with fury and abandon, and the stories both sung and shouted spanned the gamut of the black Southern experience—from snapshots of a sharecropper's reality (James Cotton's "Cotton Crop Blues") to the torment of a broken heart (Pat Hare's sadly prophetic "I'm Gonna Murder My Baby"); from celebrations of drunken release (Jackie Brenston's "Rocket 88") to carefully painted portraits of sweeping melancholy (Junior Parker's "Mystery Train," haunting even in the face of Elvis Presley's superior version also cut at Sun, two years after Parker's). If Howlin' Wolf represented the place where the soul of man never dies, then Sun surely was the place where the soul of man was expertly captured on a regular, workaday basis.

Along the way, Phillips dabbled in acoustic blues and doo-wop, gospel and barrelhouse boogie-woogie, landing a 1953 hit with the Prisonaires' lilting "Just Walking in the Rain" and recording some jump-blues instrumentals worthy of the swingmasters in California and Kansas City. The breadth and quality of his work is staggering, especially considering that the majority of it didn't see release until the late-seventies excavation of dozens of unissued Sun tapes.

During his nascent years in the music business, Phillips had numerous lawsuits leveled at his fledgling undertaking because of borrowed licks, wrongly solicited masters, and artists who didn't grasp the concept of a binding contract. Neither Howlin' Wolf nor B. B. King ever had a record issued on Sun; their work with Phillips was sold to bigger record companies. Likewise, Junior Parker, Bobby "Blue" Bland, and Little Milton hit their commercial strides only after they'd left Sun for more lucrative pastures. Phillips himself has remarked about the difficulties of being a white man in the South working closely with blacks. Yet he followed his vision, fulfilling his desire to provide an outlet for the music he cared about most.

"I feel strongly about a lot of the blues that was real true, unadulterated life as it was," he told Sun historian Martin Hawkins in 1984. "Basically, in the black music I'd heard all my life . . . there seemed to be something that was musically good and worthwhile." And for a few short years in the early fifties, Sam Phillips proved it.

Rufus Thomas looms over the history of Memphis music like an eternal ambassador of goodwill and good grooves. A resident of the city for nearly all of his eighty-one years, and a performer and disc jockey for just about as long, Thomas's career parallels the development of black music in the South—from the farms to the minstrel shows to the nightclubs; from hard blues to throbbing soul and funk. His string of hits began in the early fifties and ran through the first part of the seventies and includes a menagerie of dance classics: "Walking the Dog," "Do the Funky Chicken," "Do the Funky Penguin." Even when the hits stopped coming, Thomas kept on shimmying across concert stages in Memphis and around the globe, living up to his self-anointment as the World's Oldest Teenager.

Thomas, born March 26, 1917, was already a Beale Street club veteran in 1948 when his friend and mentor, Nat D. Williams—Memphis's first black radio personality—gave him a job at WDIA. Between spinning local and national blues hits, Thomas cut his own record in 1950 for the Texas-based Star Talent label, "I'll Be a Good Boy," recorded at Johnny Curry's Club in Memphis. The single didn't do much, and Thomas held on to his day gig at WDIA while continuing to work nights on Beale Street, emceeing an amateur show that hosted the likes of B. B. King, Bobby "Blue" Bland, Rosco Gordon, and Johnny Ace.

Thomas's initial recordings with Sam Phillips at the Memphis Recording Service were cut in 1951 and 1952; six of them were leased to Chess Records in Chicago. Three singles met the same fate as that Star Talent disc. It was "Bear Cat"—written by Phillips in 1953 as a soundalike answer to Big Mama Thornton's massive hit, "Hound Dog"—that gave Thomas his first proper release on Sun (No. 181). It was also the studio's first hit actually issued on the glowing golden-yellow label.

. . . . RUFUS THOMAS . . . .

I was born in a little town in Mississippi, not far from Collierville, in Marshall County, Mississippi. A little town called Cayce. I know little or nothing about Cayce because my parents, who were sharecroppers on a farm out there, they moved to Memphis when I was two years old, so I grew up in Memphis. I've been in Memphis ever since. Believe it or not, I've never really wanted to live any other place. Folks would ask me, "Why didn't you go to New York?" or "Why didn't you go to Chicago? Man, you're good as anybody." But I just never wanted to go out there.

When I was growing up, I went to elementary school through the fifth grade, and while I was there I played the part of a frog on Beale Street. They had a play at a theater called The Grande, and I was hopping on the stage like a frog, not knowing that in later years animals would be the reason for the bigger success that I would have in the business. Then I went to another elementary school called Porter School, but I couldn't finish the term at Porter. I had to transfer to another school because I was out of the district. In the meantime, I don't know how it popped in my mind, but I had seen some tap dancers, and lo and behold, I wanted to be a tap dancer. A fella by the name of Edwin Martin who was a schoolmate—oooh, could he dance. So I said, "I want to *learn* this." I knew a little bit about it, and I would take the little dance step that I knew and mix it up with something that I had gotten by somebody else—you might say I stole a little—and I put that together with what I knew so I got a whole brand-new dance step.

I don't know where the drive came from. All I knew is I wanted to be a tap dancer, and I wanted to be as good as I could. So I continued to work at it because during those days there was no such thing as dancing schools for blacks, so what I had to learn I had to learn on my own. Nobody could teach me. But in the meantime, I was struggling with this thing. I'd give my mama hell sometime,

Rufus Thomas, the Memphis ambassador of goodwill and good grooves

trying to get those dance steps together. Dancing out on the porch. There were some fellas who would come around and they were learning also, and I was trying to teach them the little bit that I knew. When I left the eighth grade I went to the ninth grade at Booker T. Washington High School, and that's when things really began to happen for me. I was more or less not a full-fledged tap dancer, but I had learned the craft and I was slowly becoming better. My ninth-grade history teacher was Nat D. Williams. He was sort of my mentor. He had a mind like nobody I'd ever met. He used to take me around to adult functions. I'd be the only kid in there. I guess he just wanted to show me how the other side worked. But I was always with him, right at his coattails.

The way I met him, the first rehearsal that was called at school Nat was on the stage and looked down at me and said, "What's your name?" I said, "My name's Rufus Thomas." He said, "You want to be in the ballet?" I said, "Yeah." He said, "Let me see your smile." So I had a funny little grin on my face and he said, "You got it." And from there on in we became very good friends along with him being my history teacher.

So we start to having plays at Booker T. Washington, and that was actually my start in show business. They were musicals. The first one that I was in was a minstrel show. You'd have about twelve fellas, and there would be an interlocutor. During that time, there were people like Al Jolson and Eddie Cantor. They were the well-known people at the time. They used to put that black stuff on, that black caulk on their faces, and have the lips all red. So I guess it was sort of a protest against us, the black entertainers—that they put black caulk on their faces, have the red lips and the blackface. I did that for maybe two years, the blackface. Then one day I woke up and looked in the mirror, and what did I see? I saw me. And that stuff burned your skin, anyway. It wasn't too bad going on but it was hell getting it off. But I thought, "I don't have to put this stuff on my face. My skin's already black, so why am I doing this?" And immediately I stopped using that stuff.

That was about the tenth grade, when I stopped putting that stuff on my face. I was doing comedy along with tap dancing, which actually improved my act—I could do all these things and then come behind it with a tap dance. And I was pretty good.

We had plays at that school that were so good we got to play a theater downtown. Just kids, playing the theater down there for weeks. At that time they used to have stage shows that came into the Palace Theater. They called it the Showplace of the South, and we were right along with some of the top-notch performers that came to this particular theater. We had chorus girls, we had comics, we had tap dancers, we had singers. You name it. And it was all students, I mean talent that you would not believe as a youngster.

Now I've learned my craft, so what I'm doing now is helping Nat put it together, teaching the chorus lines. In the meantime, I'm teaching Nat to dance. He was never a good dancer, but he could do a little stuff, enough to show you what he wanted done. By this time I was hot stuff, voted the most talented youngster in the school. I used to wear the big pants and the big shoes, and the big tie that would hang almost to the floor. And when I put on my stuff and changed for my tap-dancing act, I was so sharp I could stick up in concrete. I don't know why, but I commanded the attention of an audience. I was always able to hold them right there when I was onstage. And that sticks with me today. I don't feel like nobody—*nobody*—can do any more with an audience than I can. I'm not bragging, I just have that kind of faith and confidence in myself.

I didn't graduate with the "cumma cum laude" or nothing, but I had some fairly decent grades. I went to college at Tennessee State in Nashville, but I couldn't stay there. I'd never been away from home before, didn't know anything about that. So I went back home in 1935. Then I started working as a tap dancer in the various clubs around the city—[I was] the youngest one working in the clubs. There was the Cotton Club, then [its name was changed to] the Aristocrat. I worked at the Elk's Club. I worked at all the clubs in the city, doing social-club functions.

So now I'm graduated. I'm independent now, I'm on my own, out of school, out of the hands of Mama and Daddy now. I've got to get out there and hustle and get it for myself. I worked at the Brown Derby, a place in Orange Mound called the Goat Farm—fella who owned it had goats out there. So in 1935 I started an amateur night on Beale Street. Nat Williams was the emcee, the straight man, and I was the comic. This is at the Palace Theater on Beale Street. That's when I really got into the thing of doing comedy. Then Nat left to give his attention back to school. He was then teaching at Memphis State University, back when it wasn't cool for black folk to even be on campus. That shows you the kind of makeup and mind that he had. He was the only black at the school and a teacher, a history teacher. He was a smart, brilliant black man and I love him unto this day. He's the main reason for my beginning because without my beginning at Booker T. Washington working under him, it just wouldn't have been there.

I joined the Rabbit Foot Minstrels in 1936, run by Frank S. Walcott, a white fella who ran it out of Port Gibson, Mississippi. They called it a minstrel show, but it really wasn't. It was what we did in school. It was a musical. There was no blackface or that kind of stuff. I joined as a tap dancer. I got a youngster I went to elementary school with named Johnny Dowdy and taught him. We went together as a dance team. We had chorus girls, comedians, singers, dancers. A big vaudeville show, because that was the thing then. Costumes, big beautiful costumes, plume-type hats, big ol' feathers, tights, the whole works. Vegas couldn't have looked any better or done any better at the time.

We did maybe four months with that, started when it was warm and ended the show in November when it started getting really cool at night. We traveled by bus and when we'd get in town we'd get a room in some people's house because there were no hotels or anything like that for black people. We'd get a room for fifty cents a night. I think tops was seventy-five cents when you'd get into a plush house. That's how we survived out there, by living in people's houses. We'd work under a big tent, looked like a circus tent. Blacks on one side, whites on the other. You'd have an aisle that ran down the middle—that separation thing. We played Mississippi, Arkansas, occasionally we'd do a town in Tennessee, but not too often. Maybe play Louisiana, but mostly Mississippi. Johnny and I worked there until the show was over, back in 1936.

After this, I went to Nashville for a stint there, around 1937 or so. Johnny and I worked together at Kyle's Nightclub in Nashville. I waited tables also to pick up that extra money, but Johnny didn't want to wait no tables. We danced, and I'd wait tables all night. I was what you call a singing waiter, and I could hum, too. But I went back to Memphis and I don't think I left town anymore then for a while. Then I started working the nightclubs, social clubs. And Nat had left the amateur night on Beale Street in my hands. I'm the emcee now, and I go back and get a fella named Robert Counts—his stage name was Bones. He was four feet eleven. Little short dude. Funniest man you ever seen in your life. He could walk out on that stage and just stand there and be funny. He always smoked a big cigar, almost as big as he was. All the big clothes I used to wear transferred to him, because I'm the straight man now and he's the comic.

B. B. King came in from Indianola, Mississippi. He used to come to amateur night every Wednesday. Every person that got on the stage got a dollar—B. B. King was there to get that dollar. Remember, a street car was a nickel and a dollar could take you a long way then. You'd have money to take you to your day job and come back. B. B. King, Bobby Bland, Johnny Ace, Rosco Gordon, Walter Horton, they all were there and went off somewhere and did good. We had some nice people that come from there. Such wonderful talent. The musicians that used to play there used to work with Al Jackson's* big band, about thirteen pieces. That theater would be packed, people hanging off the rafters. We stayed down there about eleven years. Every Wednesday night. "Rufus and Bones" was the name of our act; we were a song-and-dance team.

The way I started writing songs was, when Johnny and I were working as a comedy team at the Elk's Club on Beale Street, there was a blues singer there by the name of Georgia Dickerson, and I used to write blues for her every week and she'd sing them. I wasn't singing. The only song I sang during that time was during our routine, the song we'd use to go into our routine. But I was writing these songs for this girl and she left town, which left that space there in the show. Now, I'd been writing for her, so I thought, "I'm going to try to sing to fill up that space." That's all there was to it. Never in my strongest imagination did I ever think that what happened would have happened. So the first song I sang was one of Lonnie Johnson's

9

*Al Jackson Sr., father of Stax/Volt and Booker T. and the MGs' drummer, Al Jackson Jr., who also produced Al Green

tunes, "Jelly Roll Baker," and it hit like a ton of bricks. The stage was kind of set up like a boxing ring—had the rope around it. And they'd walk up them steps and, boy, put money in my hand. Never throw money—they'd put money in my hand the whole time I was singing. I could *sing* that song. Then I learned other songs and I did a few love songs, like "For Sentimental Reasons," "I'm In the Mood for Love," even did "Stardust." I didn't tackle too many pop songs because I felt like that wasn't for me with all this gravel in my voice. My voice was then beginning to turn and all that gravel come into it. I couldn't sing anything sweet. The only somebody with a gravel voice that could sing sweet was Louis Armstrong, and I'm no Louis Armstrong. Then I started working with various bands around the city and started singing in the clubs.

During all this, I have a day job at American Finishing Company. Started there in 1940. [My son] Mavis was born in 1942, and [daughter] Carla born sixteen months later. I got two children now, so I've really got to work. I've got a family. So I'm doing the amateur night on Beale, working at this club, working at American Finishing eight hours, from 6:30 A.M. to 2:30 P.M., then I'd go to WDIA all across town. I used to have a show called "Hoot and Holler." I worked like that for years.

Somebody told me they were recording there at Sun and I just went. Everybody had been in there. Sam had a completely black stable then, no white artists in there at all. All black. I had cut a song in Sun in 1953 called "Bear Cat," that was the first hit for Sun, but I had done some other songs before that. I think two songs. Then Sun leased some of my songs to Chess up in Chicago. All I wanted to do was make a record. I didn't worry about the money, because at that time you'd only get a penny a record.

"Bear Cat" was a spin-off from Willie Mae Thornton's "Hound Dog"—same background music and everything, just different words. Sort of an answer to "Hound Dog." It was a big song. The first hit with a Sun label on it. I made maybe five, six hundred dollars off it. Sam made a bit more than that. But Sam wouldn't hardly tell anyone I made the first record for him that got a hit until about three years ago. They'd put us on panels together and he never did mention it. But I'd always come back and say, "Sam didn't tell you that I made the first record."

He was an arrogant bastard. He is today. Back then he had a big car, it was maybe a foreign car, a Bentley, and he'd boast about the money he made that got him this car. I said, "Yeah, but if it hadn't been for me, he wouldn't have had that car."

Thomas gave Sun its first big hit, but "Bear Cat" also prompted a lawsuit from Don Robey, whose Peacock label and Lion Music publishing company owned the copyright to the Jerry Leiber/Mike Stoller composition "Hound Dog." Phillips had to give Robey two cents per copy from the considerable sales of "Bear Cat." Another Thomas Sun single was released ("Tiger Man"/"Save That Money") but Thomas left the label in 1954. He recorded one single in 1956 for Meteor ("Easy Lovin' Plan"/"I'm Steady Holdin' On"), then found another Memphis home at Satellite, a fledgling label and studio later renamed Stax, whose first chart success arrived with a Thomas track—"'Cause I Love You," recorded in 1959 with his daughter Carla. Thomas spent the next ten or so years at the label, turning the latest dance steps of the day into pile-driving anthems such as "The Dog," "Walking the Dog," "Do the Funky Chicken," and "Do the Push and Pull."

Little Milton Campbell eventually found fame similar to that of Thomas, but he tasted hardly a drop of it during his tenure at Sun. He made his debut on the label in 1953 with "Beggin' My Baby," and a total of three singles were issued before he left in 1954. He recorded briefly with Meteor and the St. Louis-based Bobbin label (where he found his first major hit with "I'm a Lonely Man" in 1959). Milton didn't find his groove, however, until he hit Chess Records in

Chicago, where he reinvented himself as an urbane R&B crooner and helped bridge the gap between the Delta blues of his youth and Windy City soul with sixties hits such as "Blind Man," "We're Gonna Make It," and "If Walls Could Talk." He's never broken through to the mainstream, but he found his share of airspace in the South with the Mississippi-based Malaco label, where he cut the eighties cult hit "The Blues Is Alright."

..LITTLE MILTON CAMPBELL..

The legendary Ike Turner introduced me to Sun Records. See, my hometown is just outside of Leland, Mississippi, in the Delta, and Ike Turner's home was in Clarksdale. At the time I was just a local dude trying to make a name for himself. I was about eighteen. I had been playing all around, doing pretty good. I had performed with some of the greatest guys I knew as a sideman. I had performed as a guitar player and recorded some with the late Willie Love, one of the King Biscuit members. Sonny Boy Williams, Joe Willie Wilkins, I was associated with these guys. They were my mentors. I had learned so much from them, about music and the business.

Ike took me in, him and his little group. Ike would come down to my hometown and play, and sometimes I'd run into him on the road. Sometimes when musicians travel around they sort of bump into each other, and that's how I knew Ike. He had been pretty successful, because he had been associated with Jackie Brenston, "Rocket 88," things of that nature. And he knew practically everyone in the business that was doing anything at that time—all the record labels and what-have-you. Ike has been a guy that's always been pretty sharp, pretty keen, with a lot of drive and ingenuity. There was a whole bunch of guys around at that time that wanted to make records but didn't know anybody or know how or whatever. So Ike asked me if I wanted to make records, and naturally that was a goal of mine, so he was the one who took me to Sun Records and Sam Phillips.

The first session I did, I was just extremely overjoyed. The very first recording we did for Sun Records, "Beggin' My Baby," Ike is playing piano. His nephew, Jesse Knight—we called him Junior—was playing bass, and he had a drummer named Willie Sims that we called "Bad Boy." And I had one of my members with me, he played sax, C. W. Tate. So we probably did maybe three or four sessions. We didn't write anything. At that time the trend was, whoever had a hit record out, you would try to make up some lyrics as you go along and try to sound as close to that record as possible. Nowadays, it's not allowed. You'd get sued to death. Back then, you'd take the melody and the music and put some different lyrics to it and you'd get away with it. At that time B. B. King was just getting hot, Fats Domino, Chuck Willis. We had people like that to try and sound like. That's not the correct way to do it, but that's how we did it then, and sometimes you'd get extremely lucky and come up with a hit. And sometimes we did pretty good. We'd get a few bucks out of it when we'd finish the sessions, but not a hell of a lot. No royalties. That was the trend. Of course, you weren't getting much anyway. Maybe a cent per copy?

They weren't as big hits as they could've been, because at that time Sun Records was just a little small independent company. It was the same old story even then, but at least the airspace was there for you, whereas today they ignore the music. The space was there for you but it's sort of like being a little fish in a big tank. The big fish control everything, and if you're not careful, they'll eat you up. I think that was the case with Sun. Even though the airspace was there, the other big labels sort of had first preference.

Sun was like the beginning, like first grade for me. Then we went from Sun to another little independent label in Memphis, Meteor, owned by one of the Bahari brothers. So all the time I moved up another notch in my learning process—learning who I was and what I was doing. Then we got to the Bobbin label, which I helped to start in St. Louis with Oliver Sain. We recorded Albert King on the label, and Fontella Bass. The very first recording we did on the label was my "I'm a Lonely Man." During this time, this era, I was coming into my very own as far as the voice and style goes, and by the time I got to Chess I was more or less graduated. But I think I was able to let it all hang out at Sun, as far as the talent that was deep within that I would later really learn to develop.

Little Milton's last single for Sun—1954's "If You Love Me"—was among the last pure blues recordings released by Sam Phillips before the epochal July 1954 session with Elvis Presley.

Memphis-born pianist Rosco Gordon not only found success with Phillips, he remained on the Sun roster until 1958, long after Phillips had abandoned the blues for the lucrative greenery of the rock and roll market. A precocious, self-taught piano player noted for his robust, powerful rhythm, Gordon was only sixteen when he landed his own radio show on WDIA in 1951, after taking first prize at one of Rufus Thomas's famed amateur nights on Beale Street. He was quickly ushered into Phillips's studio, where he worked off and on for the next seven years.

Gordon's discography is a mess, with sessions recorded for numerous labels concurrently (and often cutting the same material for each). We know for sure, at least, that his first sides were cut with Phillips and leased first to Modern's RPM subsidiary, later to Chess. His second single for RPM, 1951's "Saddled the Cow (And Milked the Horse)," was a number 9 R&B hit, but it was 1952's "Booted," a rolling ode to the joys of getting bombed highlighted by an appropriately slurred vocal, that gave Gordon his first number one R&B hit. The flip-side, "Love You 'Til the Day I Die," marked the recording debut of Bobby "Blue" Bland, a friend of Gordon's who dueted with him on the record.

I was born April 10, 1934, in Memphis, Tennessee, raised in South Memphis on Florida Street. My mother was Idella Tobin and my father was Rosco Gordon the first. I had six sisters and one brother. I'm the youngest. I had a twin sister, she passed about four years ago, in 1992. I was self-taught on the piano, and how I got into this dumb business was, my youngest sister was taking piano lessons. When she would come home to study her lessons, I would sit on one end of the piano stool and every chord she would make I would add maybe two or three notes to it and that was how I learned the piano. I was about eight then. My parents wanted me to play spirituals. I had to go to church a lot when I was a kid. I had to go every week.

So I was playing piano with my sister for maybe two or three years. At the same time I would go to pick cotton every Saturday. Every Saturday I had to go to the cotton field to pick cotton in Arkansas, Missouri, Mississippi, anywhere. The truck would pick us up in the morning and we would go and pick cotton all day. I would sing all day, and everybody in the cotton field would try to get close to me because I would be singing. They were getting their free entertainment from me.

I left home at twelve, so as for a childhood, I didn't have too much. I went to Tinley Park, Illinois. They had a job offer on one of the railroads in Tinley Park, so these three brothers and I were supposed to leave town to go see about that job. We'd run away from home. So we're supposed to meet in a boxcar that was going north. We didn't care where it was going as long as it was getting out of Memphis. I got there first, and I was the only one that got there. We had marked the freight car we were supposed to get in, so I arrived, got in the car, and went to sleep in the freight car. I wake up in the middle of the night, that train is chugging on down the line, scared the devil out of me!

15

When I got to Tinley Park I got off the train and went to apply for the job. I got the job but I only worked four days because the work was too strenuous for me. I've always been about the same size, about one hundred twenty, one hundred thirty pounds, and as long as I was packing the rocks under the cross ties, okay, I could do that. But [the foreman] was going to put another guy and myself on a cross tie to pick up with some tongs, and I said, "No, man, I can't pick that up." So he said, "You are a man, you're getting a man's wages, you'll do a man's job." I said, "Nah, nah, I'm not going to pick that up," so he fired me. Well, I said, "If you're going to fire me, give me my money and I'll go." He said I had to go to LaSalle Street Station in Chicago to get paid, but I needed my money then. I had no money at all. I told him that and he said, "Then go back to work." Well, I made a remark. I said, "This is the first time I've been hired and fired in less time than five minutes." And he said, "Go."

But another guy there said, "If you're going to fire him then I'm going to quit, too." So together we cut people's lawns and got handouts, because we didn't have any money. I don't know how far we were from Chicago, but we had to walk to Chicago from Tinley Park, Illinois. So we go to the LaSalle Street Station to ask for our pay and we had to wait until payday! So we hung out there and slept on the sidewalks and in abandoned cars, everywhere, until we got paid. I didn't want to call my mother to let her know where I was, but I called her—the situation *made* me call her—and she told me I had an Uncle Bill there on Dearborn Street and she said to go stay there until she could send me some money to come home. So I go to his house, and when I first got there every other day he'd give me four or five dollars. After about two or three weeks it got down to two dollars, and after another three or four weeks he said, "Hey, man, you've got to get a job." This is when I called my mother and she sent me money and I went back on home and I went back to the same situation of picking cotton and singing in the fields.

In a way I didn't want to leave Chicago, because I was living the life. We had a guy on the corner of Harrison and State Street that had a frank wagon there, and we would go by there and snatch a frank and a bun and run away. After we did that for about a week, when he'd see us coming he would make us up a frank and give it to us. We were going to take it anyway, because we were hungry! At that time the supermarkets would put the fruit and produce outside, and I ate so many bananas I don't like them today. I ate so many apples that I can't eat an apple today. They give me diarrhea.

When I got back to Memphis, I had these two friends. We were inseparable. We liked to drink Mogen David wine, and on this particular Wednesday night we had no wine money, so we went to the amateur night that they had every Wednesday night on Beale Street, where Rufus Thomas was the emcee. They coaxed me to go up onstage to make the wine money. You'd get some kind of money whether you won first prize or second prize or whatever. Everybody up in the theater where we'd sit, they knew us. They called us the Miserable Three or something like that. I don't remember exactly, but I know it wasn't a pleasant name. So I go up and sing a song called "Please Throw This Old Dog a Bone," and Rufus's other emcee was named Bones, so when I was singing "Please Throw This Old Dog a Bone" he threw a great big bone up on the stage and that got me first prize. So when you win first prize, the next day, Thursday, you're on WDIA. Nat D. Williams would interview you on his show. So I went there that Thursday and everybody knew me, they'd called the radio station and sent in cards and letters and everything, so that Friday I was invited back, and I also went back that Saturday. On Monday I got my own show on WDIA. I don't remember if it was fifteen or thirty minutes, but I know it was short. I played the piano and sang. I was about sixteen, I think. I had added a drummer, Man Son—he didn't have any drums so I had to buy him a set of drums—and Raymond Thomas was the alto player. That's all I

had—drums, alto, and myself. That went on for approximate-
ly two months. I was doing mostly Nat King Cole songs and
Charles Brown and Ivory Joe Hunter. They were my idols. Still
are. So I'd play their songs and sing, and later on David James,
the station manager at WDIA, set up a deal for me to meet Sam
Phillips.

I didn't know anything about nothing then. I had no idea
that I was going to become a musician. The only reason I did it
to start with was for the wine money. That's all. I didn't have
sense enough to be nervous. The only thing I wanted to do was
sing. That's all. I didn't care who I sang for or where I sang,
that's just all I wanted to do. But I was working four or five
nights a week after the radio station, getting $125, $150, up to
$200 a night, even after I've paid the musicians! Before I went
to Sam Phillips, I had a bankroll. I'd already bought myself a
car.

Sam was very nice, though, and after everything was set up
he had this song that Courtney Harris wrote called "Booted,"
and he asked if I could play it. I said, "Yeah, I can play anything," so he gave it to me and I learned it with my band. By
then I added Billy Love to the band. We lived about two blocks
apart. See, my mother got rid of the piano because I wouldn't
play what she wanted me to play. She wanted me to play spirituals, but I wouldn't do it. I still don't want to play them,
because you can't serve two masters, and I'm really God-fearing. That was instilled in me when I was a little kid, and I still
do fear God. But I liked the sound that I made better. But she
got rid of the piano, so I would go to Billy's house periodical-
ly—two or three times a week—and I would learn from him.
Billy was maybe four or five years older than me. He had so
much talent. If you couldn't learn from him you couldn't learn
from anybody. He would show you note for note how to make
the chord. But I didn't want to make the chord that he sub-
scribed for me to play, so what I would do was make a bigger
chord out of the chord that he'd teach me. He'd teach me a

three- or four-note chord, and I would make it six or just as many as I could. I've got pretty large hands so I would stretch my hands as far as I could to find a note that fit that chord.

But anyway, after I recorded "Booted" for Sam he said I'd have to have another side. At this time Bobby Bland was my chauffeur. His mother had a restaurant on Third Avenue in Memphis, and we would always congregate there—the musicians and I would meet there and eat his mother's cooking. His mother was a fabulous cook. And I knew Bobby's cousin. Bobby's cousin was my driver, but this particular night he couldn't go, so he said, "My cousin Bobby will take you to the job," and that's how I met Bobby. This night we were working in Arkansas, we still had only the one song, and we were on our way to a gig in Arkansas, and on the way Bobby was singing, "Well, it's 'fore day in the morning, I got these early morning blues." I said, "This thing is wrong, man, I'm supposed to be *your* chauffeur." But I had written a song called "Love You 'Til the Day I Die," for the other side after I found out Bobby could sing. He said, "I got the voice, but I don't have any timing." I said, "All you got to do is say, 'One–two–three–four—SING— two–three–four—SHUT UP—two–three–four,'" and so on.

But this night in Arkansas I put Bobby on the stage because I was an avid dice shooter. I loved to shoot dice. I don't shoot dice now, but I loved to at that time. So I put Bobby on the stage that night and went to the dice table. I shot dice all night and nobody bothered me, so Bobby must've been all right. I don't know how he did, but nobody came to me to sing, so Bobby must've been all right. I told him that I had to write this song, and Bobby and I did it at Sun.

So the first thing I know, I'm a big act. There was this guy named Littlefield that came from Chicago who took me to my first job, at B. B. Beeman's auditorium in Atlanta, Georgia. I had never been on no professional gigs before. All of this was happening in less than two months' time. I had hit records, the next song I wrote was "No More Doggin'," and it's selling today like it was just released yesterday. But that Atlanta show was miserable. Little Esther and Mel Walker were on the show and I think Johnny Otis had the band, and I did three shows and had to do "Booted" back to back on each show. That put me out with "Booted." I haven't sung it since and I still don't do it. I was so sick of it. You sing the same song once, then you sing it again, and then one more time. That's all I did. I said, "I know other songs I want you to play," and Otis said, "This is your hit record and this is all I'm going to play. If you don't like this, get your own band."

So after that show I got back to Memphis and I got my own band. Man Son played the drums, Willie Wilkes was on tenor, and Richard Sanders on baritone, and I'd just pick up a guitar player. Tuff Green played bass on most of my recordings, and Billy Duncan, a tenor player. Pat Hare played on "Shoobie Oobie" and a lot of my things. I liked Pat Hare. Any time I wanted a guitar player, if I could get Pat Hare, he was my choice. He had a sound. That solo on "Shoobie Oobie" stays in my head all the time, but I can't find a guitar player today of his calibre nowhere.

The people in the band were mostly neighbors. We would all go to Sunbeam Mitchell's Club Handy and I would meet a lot of musicians. They didn't want to play with me, though, because I wanted to play my way and they wanted to play what they called "right," but any way you enjoy your music is right. Twelve bars, four bars, one bar, half a bar, whatever, if that's the way you want to do it, that's the way you want to do it. I didn't want to play the other people's songs. After I got my own records out there I wanted to play my own records, so the musicians, when I would go on stage, everybody would have to go to the bathroom! Everybody but the drummer, and then sometimes he would go and there'd be nobody on the stage but me. But I met a lot of musicians and I put my local band together—the band

I recorded with. But they had jobs in Memphis so they couldn't leave, so I let Billy Love put another band together. I had one band I recorded with and another band that I traveled with.

What I remember about Ike Turner was, he came to town with the Bihari brothers. He came alone and set up all the musicians that they were going to record, and after he set up everything the Bihari brothers come and they rented places to record. B. B. King recorded "Three O'Clock Blues" at Tuff Green's house, and I recorded "No More Doggin'" and "Marie" at his house.

We were working in Arkansas one night, my band and I, and after we did "No More Doggin'" and "Marie" that day, when it was time to go to the gig, I couldn't find anybody. I called everybody and I couldn't find anybody, so I called Willie Wilkes's wife, her name was Mary, and she said Ike Turner had picked up Wilkes and the whole band and that they hadn't finished recording yet. I said, "What?" I hopped in the car and went to Tuff Green's house and I heard my "No More Doggin'" and this strange voice singing it. I said, "What the devil is this?" and banged on the door. I had to get in there and find out what this is! So I got in there and apologized to Tuff for knocking on his door, you know, the way I banged on it. But I get in there and Ike Turner is singing "No More Doggin'," with *my* band—got the whole band in there singing *my* song. I said, "Hey, man, what is this?" He said, "Aw, I just wanted to see how it sounded with me doing it." I said, "That's my song," and I started to hurt Ike. But I thought, "No, that won't make any sense." I picked up my musicians and questioned them, saying, "Why would you want to do this to me?" and they said, "We're just like you. Money's money, man. You paid us to do a session? Well, we're going to get paid for *two* sessions." Well, they didn't get paid for that second session. I broke that up.

The last time I saw Ike Turner, I had gone to A&M [University] over in Arkansas and he was working over there. He'd brought his first wife [Bonnie Turner] with him, his whole band, and Tina Turner. That was the first time I'd seen Tina. But his wife was just crying, just going out of her head. She said, "Ike Turner's quitting me." I said, "What's wrong?" She said, "He's quitting me for *her*," for Tina. When I looked at the comparison, I said, "Hey." His wife was good-looking, but she wasn't talented. The only talent she had was for having babies, so I said to myself, "I don't blame him."

If Gordon was one of the more consistent hitmakers to cross the threshold of the Memphis Recording Service, he was also a source of almost constant legal wrangling for Phillips. The problems with Gordon were rooted in a dispute between Phillips, Chess Records chief Leonard Chess, and the Bihari brothers at Modern/RPM over "Rocket 88," a huge hit in 1951 by Jackie Brenston's Delta Cats (featuring Ike Turner) and the first big seller recorded by Phillips.

He had already been placing recordings by B. B. King and Joe Hill Louis with RPM through a handshake agreement, but he sent the "Rocket 88" dubs to Chess, hoping to expand his operation. When the song hit the number one R&B slot in June of 1951, the Biharis were infuriated. Matters were made worse that same year when Phillips sent the initial recordings of Howlin' Wolf ("How Many More Years," "Baby Ride With Me") to both Chess and RPM; he later sold Wolf's contract to Chess at the same time that Ike Turner ushered the artist into the studio to re-record those songs for RPM.

Enter Gordon, who, like countless blues artists before him, especially Lightnin' Hopkins and John Lee Hooker, would cut songs with anyone who paid him, regardless of prior contractual commitments. Both Phillips and the Biharis were working with Gordon simultaneously in the early fifties, with Sam sending the results to Chess and the Biharis issuing them on RPM. Such was the case with "Booted," which was issued by both Chess and RPM. A lawsuit was filed against Leonard Chess by the Biharis, but even after the two parties came to an agreement in which Chess would work exclusively with Howlin' Wolf and Modern/RPM with Gordon, Phillips still had problems with the prolific pianist. Phillips rival Don Robey, head of Duke Records in Houston, slapped yet another Gordon-related lawsuit on Sun.

Gordon says he was unaware at the time of the brouhaha between Chess and RPM concerning "Booted." He fesses up, however, to the hubbub surrounding "The Chicken," issued on Sun at the tail end of 1955.

. . . . *GORDON* . . . .

I found out about all of it after I'd signed "The Chicken" over. See, what happened was, Bill Harvey worked with Don Robey, and Bill was staying over at the hotel at Club Handy, where we rehearsed all the time. It was free to rehearse there and we always had an audience. Bill listened to us and said, "I want to tape 'The Chicken' and play it back for you." So he got it on tape and played it back, but he passed it on to Don Robey. I was working out at the Crystal Ballroom and Robey came out there and asked if that was my song, and I said, "yeah," and he said, "I'll give you two hundred dollars to sign it over to me." We went from $200 up to $460, so I signed it over to him. I didn't know anything about rights or copyrighting or anything. I was just trying to get all the money I could any way that I could get it. I wasn't getting any royalties and I wasn't getting paid properly, so if you want me to do a session, if you've got my price I'll do it. So I signed it over to Robey, and that was how he got to sue Sam. I think he sued him for $40,000 or $45,000.

I don't know what happened to the Biharis. I know what happened with Leonard Chess, though—why he wouldn't have anything to do with me. He said I would record for anybody and they didn't want an artist who would do that. So I only did the one record for Leonard.

Although Gordon's biggest hit was a drinking song, and his best unissued Phillips track was the sloppy-drunk anthem "Decorate the Counter," he claims he was abstaining during the period, despite his early taste for Mogen David and his slurred, red-eyed delivery on those frantic cuts.

. . . . **GORDON** . . . .

Everybody drank but me. I still don't drink. Only during the time of the amateur nights did I drink. After that I cut it loose. I was working at a club called Dora's Nightspot in Mason, Tennessee, and a guy came up there with some white lightning. And I thought with this sweetening in it, I didn't think it was going to knock me out. So I drank some of that, and on my way home somebody else had to drive the car. I had my head out the window and I was vomiting all the way back to Memphis. It happened to me twice, and after that I said, "I'm not going to drink anything that makes you sick behind it."

Another time, I met this girl in Oakland, an angel, and she drank champagne. After the gig she wanted champagne. So I got a bottle of champagne. We went out to eat first, then we went back to the hotel with the champagne. So we take a shower and pop the cork on the champagne. And I got drunk on that champagne and I missed her! I didn't have anything to do with this angel. And I said, "Hey, this is foolish, sitting here and getting drunk." After that, no more drink. I mean no more whatsoever.

As far as drinking and doing drugs, when I look out there and see that audience and see them enjoying my music, I'm high as a kite, man. That's my high right there, when I see you enjoying my music and clapping your hands and I know that this came from *me*—the arranging, the writing, the everything, I don't need nothing else. I can't understand these people that need to get high to go out on the stage. Just look at your audience!

Rosco Gordon, Sam Phillips, and friend celebrate the release of Gordon's 1955 Sun single "The Chicken." (Center for Southern Folklore Archives)

Booted or not, Gordon succeeded during the early fifties in helping to define the boozy, loose-limbed sound of jump blues the way Sam Phillips always heard it—not with the uptown swing of the big bands behind Wynonie Harris, Roy Brown, or Joe Turner, but with a driving, primal wallop that was anything but urbane. Gordon signed on with Duke in 1952 but found only marginal success over a handful of fine singles. He returned to Phillips in 1955 and made his proper Sun debut that year with "Just Love Me Baby" (Sun No. 227). By the next year, Gordon would be the only blues artist under contract to Phillips, but after the dispute with Duke over "The Chicken," Phillips lost interest in him despite issuing singles on this troublesome artist as late as 1958.

Gordon would later hook up with Vee-Jay Records in Chicago for the biggest pop hit of his career—1960's "Just a Little Bit," built around a snaky riff written by Jimmy McCracklin that made it a natural cover for frat bands, surf groups, and anyone else looking for an unshakably catchy groove thing. The song made it less than halfway up the Top 100 and was actually a bigger hit for Roy Head ("Treat Her Right"), whose 1965 version cracked the Top 40.

TWO

Elvis and the Kings of Western Bop

Let's dispense with the hyperbole and mythology and romance surrounding Elvis Presley and his first recordings and look instead at a few facts. Rockabilly was born in the early part of July 1954, at Sam Phillips's Sun studio on 706 Union Avenue in Memphis, Tennessee. It was the collaborative creation of four men: Phillips, Presley, bassist Bill Black, and guitarist Scotty Moore, a stylistic hodge-podge that synthesized blues, country, bluegrass, and pop into something different. After witnessing its birth—in particular, after Presley, Black, and Moore transformed Bill Monroe's "Blue Moon of Kentucky" into something that swung a lot harder than the bluegrass master's old maudlin waltz—Phillips told the musicians, "Hell, that's different. That's a pop song now, nearly 'bout."

Actually, what it was, was rock and roll, but before it picked up the name, the hybrid concocted by Phillips and the Presley trio was referred to in the trade papers as rockabilly. Its glory days were relatively brief—born in '54, at its commercial peak in '56, pretty much a dead dog by the turn of the sixties, co-opted by the honky-tonkers in Nashville but soon to be absorbed into the nascent Brit-rock rumblings of the Beatles. Because of the raw country sound that lurked beneath its popping guitar, slapback bass, and blues-soaked swing—not to mention the tape-manipulated echo pioneered by Phillips—rockabilly was a regional music popular mostly in the South and Southwest, although it did break nationally on rare occasions.

Few artists ever managed to get a slab of rockabilly anywhere on the *Billboard* charts, though, and the ones who did seldom pulled it off twice. The genre produced a few visionaries—most notably Buddy Holly—but most of them took Elvis's lead and broke free of rockabilly's sonic constrictions as soon as they mastered its principles. (As for Jerry Lee Lewis, he transcended the genre the day he entered Sun to cut his first single. Calling him a rockabilly is like calling John Wayne a cowboy actor.) The ones who couldn't adapt either disappeared, fell into the country scene in Nashville, or beat a path to Europe, where genuine American rockabilly was a rare and precious commodity. Virginia rocker Gene Vincent, the man who cut the 1956 Elvis soundalike "Be-Bop-A-Lula," spent the duration of his career as an expatriate, feeding scraps of Southern rock and roll to European audiences. Even in the 1990s, aging rockabillies are playing festivals and club gigs in England, France, Germany, Switzerland, Japan, and beyond, earning more money than they ever did making records for the myriad labels that popped up in the post-Presley world.

Sun wasn't the only label in Memphis that concentrated on rockabilly, nor did it snare every local act worth hearing. Meteor issued some fine rockabilly and jumping country at the same time as Sun, although some of Meteor's best work was produced by former Sun vets such as Charlie Feathers and Malcolm Yelvington. One of the city's finest hillbilly-bop ensembles, Johnny Burnette's Rock and Roll Trio, didn't pass an audition with Sam Phillips. They wound up recording their seminal rockabilly sides such as "Train Kept A-Rollin'" and "Tear It Up" in Nashville for Coral, the early home of Buddy Holly. Roy Orbison's best stuff came only after he left Sun, where he was seldom allowed to indulge his penchant for ballads. Still, with few exceptions—Holly, Vincent, Eddie Cochran—the greatest rockabilly was produced in Memphis, and the bulk of that was cut at Sun, by artists who have either entered the pantheon of rock history or merely titillated the most rabid of the music's hard-core faithful. (And the rockabilly crowd is a rabid bunch, to say the least.)

Although most of Sun's issued 45s were devoted to rockabilly and its country-bop kin, hours of recordings remained unreleased until the late seventies, when the British Charly label began its massive excavation of Sun's tape archive. For collectors and aficionados, the Charly collections were revelatory affairs: Suddenly one-hit wonders like Carl Perkins were revealed to be masters of the form, with some of their best material buried in scintillating alternate takes and songs that, for one reason or another, were deemed unusable by Phillips. And suddenly, no-hit wonders like Sonny Burgess were shown to be fiendishly rocking madmen with catalogs full of rompers, stompers, and hellfire shouters.

Of course, in comparison to the work of rock and roll's greatest early artists—Elvis, Jerry Lee, Chuck Berry, and Buddy Holly—the discographies of these Sun lunatics are somewhat underwhelming. What they reveal most is that rockabilly is perhaps the most limited genre in music history, comprised mostly of countless calls to "rock rock rock" and "go, man, go," endless hours of sub-Presley hiccupping vocals, and innumerable attempts to master the fingerpicking guitar verities of Scotty Moore. Certain distinct personalities did emerge from the chaos and insanity of the era, including rockabilly standard-bearer Charlie Feathers (maybe the strangest vocalist of the genre) and the raving Billy Lee Riley, one of the few rockabillies at Sun who really should've been a contender.

What those collections also reveal is that of the thousands of rockabilly sides both immediately issued and unreleased until the archival boom, the finest were cut under the guidance of Sam Phillips. In his willingness to simply let the tape roll, to record seemingly anyone who had the balls to walk into his studio, Phillips managed to capture a moment in rock history when white men were grappling with the influence of the blues and how it figured into the country music of their raising—when the best of them believed that it was actually possible to rock harder than Elvis Presley.

Few men ever pulled it off, but Phillips offered a home to the ones who tried and the two who succeeded: Jerry Lee Lewis, whose greatness eclipsed rockabilly, rock and roll, and country-and-western and encompassed the entire history of American music; and Carl Perkins, the quintessential rockabilly in that he mastered its themes and concepts—and even introduced some of them along the way—yet never figured out how to apply them to anything else, how to move them into new and different territory (something that Billy Lee Riley managed with the early-seventies white-soul shot "I've Got a Thing About You Baby"). Perkins, more than any other artist—even, you could argue, more than Elvis—provides the archetype for rockabilly in his powerful, biting guitar

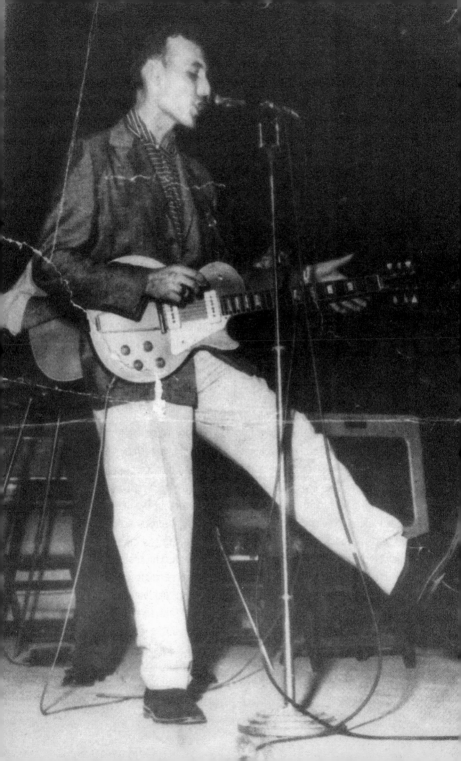

work, his gritty, evocative Tennessee twang, and his picture-perfect snapshots of Southern life. (I'm thinking especially of "Dixie Fried," not an unearthed outtake but a 1956 B-side, a saga of roadhouse madness so raw, ragged, and inherently Southern that the thought of a deejay spinning it on a pop or even a country radio station would be like a gang of liquored-up hillbillies crashing into Carnegie Hall to lend vocal support to *La Bohème*.) But after providing much of rockabilly's sound and vocabulary, Perkins hit the same creative dead end as most of the men he inspired.

That doesn't lessen his importance or reduce the impact of his work at Sun. Instead, Perkins typifies the plight of the music and the artists who made it. Rockabilly never really died. In one form or another it's always been around—in the sixties hoodoo boogie of Ronnie Hawkins; the seventies country-pop of Billy Swan; the post-punk savagery of the Cramps; and in revivalist goofballs from Crazy Cavan to the Stray Cats. The music's insatiable cult continues to grow as boutique labels in the United States and abroad ferret out every last rockabilly record worth hearing—or not worth even forgetting. It's a testament to Sam Phillips's greatness, to his genius, that the ones worth remembering were cut at Sun.

. . . . S C O T T Y   M O O R E . . . .

When I came out of the navy in January of '52 I started playing around with different bunches on the weekends. Nobody seemed to have a group with the same guys all the time. Even myself, I would go out and book a club and *then* go get a band together for that weekend, so you'd have all kinds of different combinations. Whatever you did, you had to play whatever the hits were in pop, country, and R&B—mainly stuff that people could dance to. I did that for a little while and I thought, "This is not the way to do it. You need to get a group together and stay together for a while." I had played with Bill Black a few times in different things, and knew a lot of different guys, so I tried to get a group together. It seemed at that point that the easiest route

Don't even think of stepping on the shoes:
Carl Perkins during a mid-fifties concert.
(Center for Southern Folklore Archives)

was in country. That's the reason for the name—the Starlight Wranglers.

So I put that group together, and Bill started with me in that. I don't think we had a style. We were just more or less trying to ape the best we could the things we'd hear on the radio. Everybody called the music honky-tonk back then, but even though we had a western group and dressed accordingly, we still did other songs. But we'd do them with country instruments and a country feel to it.

And after we'd been together for a while, I thought that to get some better bookings and such, we needed to get on the radio. And we did get a radio show, and then I thought we needed to get a record out so we can get played on the radio and make another step up, and that's how I come about meeting Sam Phillips. I found out that Sam owned a recording studio and also had a record label, so I went to see him and we went in and auditioned for him. He was trying a little bit of everything at the time, just looking for something that would make some money. So he finally cut one record on us and put that out. It got a little airplay around Memphis and sold maybe a dozen records.

∅

The Starlight Wranglers, led by Lefty Frizzell disciple Doug Poindexter, debuted on Sun in May 1954 with "No She Cares No More for Me"/"My Kind of Carryin' On," a merely average slice of fiddle-driven honky-tonk with a fine, if unspectacular, pair of solo breaks by Moore.

. . . . *M O O R E* . . . .

Sam and I became friends after we cut the record, and I would go down almost every day in the afternoon when I'd get off work and sit next door in the cafe there with Sam and drink coffee and talk about what's being played on the radio and different styles of music. I think we were both searching. I think we both felt there needed to be something different, but nobody knew what. The whole music business was sort of in a low ebb back then—pop, everything, it just seemed to be down. There wasn't very much excitement going on.

So one day we were talking and his secretary brought up Elvis's name. He had been in there to make a record for his mother. And I worried Sam to death for a couple weeks to get ahold of him, and he finally got her to give me his number and I called him. He came over to my house and we just sat and he played. It seemed like he knew every song in the world. Bill lived a few doors down from me and he came over and listened for a while and after he left I called Sam and said, "The boy has a decent voice, knows all the songs, has good timing." And he said it sounded like we should give him a shot. He said, "I'll call him and get him to come into the studio tomorrow night. He said, "Just you and Bill come in. We don't need the whole band. I just want a little bit of background noise to see how it sounds on tape." And so we did and we went in, and, gosh, we ran through I don't know how many songs. Different styles, tempos, ballads, and during a break he started cutting up and singing "That's All Right" and I fell in with him, playing along with it. Sam heard it through the door, because the studio door was open, and he came out and said, "What are y'all doing?" We said, "Ah, just goofing around." And he said, "Well, goof around some more. Let me see what it sounds like." We were just like jamming, not trying to do anything. Just jamming, just cutting up. And the rest, as they say, is history.

"Blue Moon of Kentucky" came about the same way. After we did "That's All Right," Sam said, "Okay, we have to have a B-side," and again we went in and everybody was scratching their brains trying to think of songs to try. And this time Bill—again during the break—started "Blue Moon of Kentucky." It was originally a waltz, but he started singing it up-tempo in a high falsetto voice, just mimicking Bill Monroe. Elvis knew the song so he started and we all just fell in again.

Everything we did on Sun was done the same way. We had absolutely no material going in. We'd just go in and start kicking things around. Sam would mention some of the R&B stuff he had done, and we'd try some of that. You know, "That's All Right" was just something Elvis had heard on the radio and knew, but every session we did on Sun was done the same way—just through trial and error until something would just finally click. You didn't know what you'd come out with. And there were a few times when you didn't get anything, and you'd just come back the next day or two.

Radio play for "That's All Right" was phenomenal, and Sam couldn't get records pressed fast enough. When he first started pressing them he had five thousand back-ordered just from local orders. I think in the back of our minds Bill and I thought it was just a one-record thing, a fluke. Because it was so different from everything else that was out there. But you still had to go for what you had.

I guess after the first record made so much noise different artists started going in and getting auditions with Sam—guys who tried to sound like Elvis. Like I said, we thought the business in general needed something different, but nobody knew what and it was a fluke. Like the first record, we figured we'd go in and Sam will say, "Okay, I'll take a chance on Elvis and we'll get a full band in and start cutting something," but it just didn't work that way. And it may not have worked if he had done that. Who knows? From the radio reaction, we figured we don't need anything else.

*

The first disc jockey to spin the Elvis single (actually, it was an acetate of what would be Sun No. 209, released on July 19, 1954) was Dewey Phillips, no relation to Sam Phillips but a close friend, a one-time business partner and kindred spirit. Dewey's WHBQ program "Red Hot and Blue" was maybe the most insane, inspired, and inspiring radio show in the history of the medium—a chaotic, cacophonous train wreck of primo blues, country, and gospel interspersed with Dewey's manic voice-overs and hipster, booze-fueled patois. Memphis radio was already plugged in to the power of the blues via WDIA and disc jockeys such as Rufus Thomas and Nat D. Williams (plus regular live spots from bluesmen B. B. King and Rosco Gordon). "Red Hot and Blue," though, was something different, from the varied mix of the programming to the sheer intensity of Dewey's passion and love for the music. Perhaps even more significant, "Red Hot and Blue" was drawing both white *and* black listeners—listeners like Jim Dickinson, a producer, musician, and Memphis iconoclast who was among the last artists to record at Sun before its sale in 1969.

. . . . *JIM DICKINSON* . . . .

Think about Elvis listening to Dewey Phillips on the radio, just like me. He's six, seven years older, but basically he's in the same place: This white kid fascinated by a black thing that was forbidden. And there was this crazy guy on the radio giving it to you and telling you it's a hit. People lose sight of that. They see Dewey and his role in reverse. The only time you hear about Dewey, they say he's the guy who played Elvis on the radio for the first time. Well, what they assume when they say that is that he didn't know who Elvis was. And he *did* know Elvis, and not only did he know Elvis, Elvis, of course, knew *him.* And many of Elvis's ideas had been formed by listening to Dewey. Where the hell else did he hear the black records? Elvis Presley was in awe of Dewey Phillips, as he should have been. And as he was of Sam. And while he was in awe of those men, he performed magic.

I saw Elvis in '56, both performances in Memphis, at the Ellis Auditorium and at Russwood Park, and anyone who saw Elvis and said they were inspired to have a career in music is lying, because seeing him was like seeing something that wasn't human. Nobody in their right mind could look at Elvis Presley and think that they could do what he was doing, because it was *that strange*. But Billy Lee Riley and Sonny Burgess? When I saw them I thought, "Hell, I could do that. These guys are just rednecks singing black music and having a good time. I could do that." But Elvis Presley was superhuman. There was something in the way that he walked onstage that was beyond anything you could conceive of ever doing. It was just that cool. And of course, he wasn't unique in Memphis. There were people in Memphis in 1956 who looked and acted like Elvis. He represented a lifestyle that already existed. But he just *glowed*.

I saw the Beatles on their first tour, I've seen the Rolling Stones in all of their incarnations, seen Dylan—I never saw anything like Elvis Presley. Just the way he walked on the stage. He didn't even have to sing. And you lose sight of it in terms of contemporary society, but what he was doing was completely revolutionary and liberating. Just shaking his leg— just the simple act of shaking his fucking leg—began the whole sexual revolution and changed the way every man on earth walked, talked, and combed his hair. *To this day*. He became the most recognizable human being on the face of the earth. There's something special there. Whether Sam Phillips saw it— surely he saw it—but whether he inspired it, whether he magnified it, God only knows.

*

Between July 1954 and August 1955, five singles were released on Sun by Elvis, Scotty, and Bill over which the trio both established and perfected the rockabilly formula—the popping guitar runs and frantically slapped bass; the chooging rhythms that propel "Good Rockin' Tonight," "Milkcow Blues Boogie," and "Mystery Train"; the arsenal of vocal tricks at Presley's disposal, which

A mid-fifties shot of Sam Phillips and Elvis Presley fooling around in the Sun studio. (Center for Southern Folklore Archives)

ranged from the implied threat in his leering "Baby Let's Play House" to the silken croon of "You're a Heartbreaker." Most of the songs were regional hits, and two—"Baby Let's Play House" and "I Forgot to Remember to Forget"—cracked *Billboard*'s country-and-western Top 10. National exposure via radio shows such as the "Louisiana Hayride" and the "Big D Jamboree" boosted the trio's profile, and the national press began to roll after Presley's alliance with carny huckster Tom Parker.

When Parker lined up a deal with RCA (with whom he had worked with other clients such as Eddy Arnold and Hank Snow), Phillips sold Elvis's contract in 1955 for a then-unprecedented $35,000. The remaining Sun masters recorded by Presley—tracks such as "Trying to Get to You," "Just Because," "Blue Moon," and "I'll Never Let You Go (Little Darlin')"—trickled out in 1956 on various RCA albums and EPs, and the label quickly reissued the five Sun singles.

Phillips has said repeatedly that he has never regretted letting go of Elvis. Certainly his label was in dire need of the cash (Phillips having bought brother Jud's interest in the label shortly before the RCA deal), and Phillips was sure that recent Sun signees Carl Perkins and Johnny Cash would do for him what Elvis did before. And besides, it's hard to imagine that Phillips and Presley could've bettered "Mystery Train," Elvis's last Sun single.

. . . . **DICKINSON** . . . .

People think Sam was foolish to sell Elvis's contract, but I disagree. I think Sam was recording an idea, and that idea was almost gone, and in fact you can only see two or three little instances of it after Elvis left Sam, because Elvis was headed into pure pop music. And that's not what Sam was doing. Sam was recording an idea.

That's what to me is so vulgar about Graceland now—not the novelty shops and the tourist aspect of it, but the fact that the idea of Elvis is not there anymore. They've changed it so radically. It's all in real poor taste and it's real trashy redneck stuff, but it's no longer Elvis's poor taste, you know what I mean? It's not like the man wasn't a damn artist! Where is the art? They don't want you to see that, because it's still basically left of center. It will always be a mystery.

The damn world changed, and as a child watching it happen, it didn't cross my mind that it was anything out of the ordinary until I left Memphis and went to Texas and realized just what I had seen.

0

If Elvis's first recordings provided an awakening for white kids like Dickinson, they also sounded something of a death knell for the blues artists who provided the label's early hits.

. . . . T H O M A S . . . .

In 1954, Elvis came to Sun, and when Elvis came, Sam discarded all of the black artists that were there, including me. I don't know what he thought. Evidently he felt that—and this is me in my head, trying to think for him—that maybe blacks and whites couldn't do it together. Maybe he thought that way, and if he did, he found out that was incorrect. Not right. A bunch of hogwash. Because a few years later, me and Carla met a fella named Robert Talley who told us about Stax and took us down there. It was just one accord at Stax—to make music. If you were a good musician and a good singer, you got a chance here. Color had nothing to do with it.

They say Elvis used to go up and down Beale Street in the clubs. I never saw Elvis in a club. Never saw him on Beale Street. I'm not saying he wasn't there, but I never saw him there. But I played Elvis's music on the radio. The only black disc jockey playing his music on WDIA. David James, who was white, was the program director at WDIA. He thought that he could think for black folk. Ain't no one person can think for all people. So I'm playing Elvis and he stops me from playing

Elvis. Said black folks don't like Elvis. He was running the operation, so what could I do? I want to keep my job, so I don't play him.

But we had the Starlight Revues and Goodwill Revues that WDIA used to have for handicapped children, because they didn't have any way of getting to school, no way of even trying to get an education. If you were handicapped, you were just *there*. No teachers to teach you. So we'd put these shows on, all to raise funds to provide for these kids. And George Klein had brought Elvis backstage at one of our Goodwill Revues at Ellis Auditorium. I was playing the part of an Indian on that particular program. When Elvis was backstage, my little daughter, who was three years old at the time, pulled on him and said, "You my boyfriend," and he sat down, talked to her, and they made a picture of her sitting on his knee.

Now, everything is going, the show is going good, and one of the fellas who was in charge, like a station manager, wanted to show Elvis onstage close to the front of the show. I said "Don"—Don Kern was his name—"don't do that. If you put Elvis up there in the front of the show, the show's over. Don't do that." I guess he had the mentality of David James. But I said, "If black folks see Elvis, that's it. Put him on at the end of the show." But I took Elvis by the hand and led him onstage, and just like that, he got on that stage and did one of those moves, and the show was over. People were clamoring and carrying on, trying to get to that man. And the next day I went back to playing Elvis.

. . . . LITTLE MILTON . . . .
As a small independent label with all the racial things going on at that time, I'm sure Sam was looking at the popularity of the music—you know, what was going to be more popular for him

in a Southern city, in a Southern region. He himself said he's been criticized over a long period of time about being in love with the black music and blacks in general. Of course, they didn't use that word. They used a different word. They used the *N* word. But that's the reality and it happens.

Unfortunately nobody wants to talk about the racial thing, that the music was racist. Everybody forgets the thing that the whole thing [is about] and that's the soul, the realism of the music itself. So I think Sam was thinking, "I got a chance to shake this, and the money is coming in, so I'm gone."

Sam has been called a rebel; he's been called everything that you would call someone who feels he's in control of himself. He was a very strong believer in what he believed in, and he did basically what he wanted to do. And any time you run into anybody that does that, I think they're going to be criticized. I don't know what kind of decisions he made, like who in the hell he would invite out to his house for dinner. I don't know a thing about that. But I know that he let a lot of people be exposed that probably back then, being from the little surrounding communities such as mine, never would've been recorded. So you can't say that everything he did was unfair or bad toward those of us that did record for the label.

There are some things he's said and done in some recent interviews, though, that I felt were a little distasteful. He just never seems to think back farther than Jerry Lee Lewis, Elvis, or Johnny Cash. He never seems to think about putting in all these nice interviews that he also did—the Little Miltons, the Ike Turners, the Rufus Thomases, the Junior Parkers, and people like that. We were there. We were basically the foundation that started it all, but he seems to forget that period. He gets amnesia when he gets to that. And for that, I don't go along with him. That's the only thing, to me, that's distasteful about Sam Phillips.

Why did Sam keep me at the label? I'm the one he wasn't *paying* and you *always* keep something that's free. But Sam, he was a great person. I don't have anything against him because I got so much knowledge from him. He used to say, "What you're playing, nobody in the world is going to play that but you. It's not blues, it's not pop, it's not rock. So what I'm going to call it is Rosco's Rhythm." But after I did "Booted," it stayed on the charts for thirteen weeks and Sam only gave me $100. That's all I got for that record. Song was selling over 100,000 copies a day and he gave me $100. I was with Sam for eight years and I bet you I didn't get $300 from him that whole period. He gave me like twenty-five dollars or fifty here and there, sometimes he gave me nothing. For me being that age, that was pretty good. I had been making eight, ten dollars a day in the fields, so when you get $100 or $75, that's a lot of money, especially back then.

Elvis and I never had a social relationship, but he would always come to my sessions and to my rehearsals at Club Handy. I don't know how he found out where I was rehearsing at, or when I was rehearsing, but he was always there. He'd sit down, cross his legs, and I'd look back around and he'd be gone. Listen to any slow thing he did, and you'll hear it—you'll hear the phrases that I made that he copied. Listen to my slow, melodic things—"Let Him Try," "A Girl to Love." Elvis Presley stole a lot of things from me from that one song, "Let Him Try." I never noticed it until I was on this radio show a few years ago called "Vision to Version," and the disc jockey would play one of my songs and then play one of Elvis's and say, "Listen to this and you'll hear yourself in there."

Elvis wanted me to play behind him, but Sam said, "Naw, Rosco can't play that stuff." This was in '54, before he recorded anything or was anything, so I didn't give it another thought. He wanted me to play on "That's All Right," his first record.

Now what musician in the world, what artist who ever sat down with an instrument in his hand, can't play twelve bars? But Sam said I couldn't play that stuff, so I didn't get on the record.

I'll tell you something about Sam. Back in 1981, 1982, I went to Europe for a month and I got almost $150,000 for twenty-two days over there. So I think when I come back, and I can afford to do my own record on my own label. So I wrote Sam a letter from London or somewhere and explained to him that I wanted him to come to Sun. I said, "I don't want you to turn no dials on no instruments or nothing, I just want you in the studio. You're my inspiration." And he said, "Okay, I'll gladly do it."

Well, all right. When I come back from Europe I call him from New York and let him know when I'll be there. He said, "When you get to the studio it won't cost you nothing," so here's what I do. They're giving B. B. King an award, so I go to this award thing and I see Sam. We have our picture taken. I see everybody down there—Rufus, Jerry Lee Lewis, Charlie Rich; everybody. So the next day, I had the studio for one o'clock, and Sam said to call him at about twelve. And to this day I'm still trying to get in touch with Sam. The studio cost me $2,500 to record that thing, the studio and the musicians. I put his first big dollar in his pocket, and what was wrong with him just coming to the studio to just inspire me? But he didn't do it.

But still, he's a great producer. The greatest. I've never seen, heard, or worked with anybody with one-tenth of the knowledge that he has about the recording thing. He knows what he wants. If I give you what you want, good, bad, or whatever the outcome is, I at least gave you what you wanted. And see, by him knowing what he wanted, and with Dewey Phillips on the radio station, if he got what he wanted, Dewey was going to play the hell out of it.

Except for a few years in the mid-sixties, Roland Janes has worked with Sam Phillips for close to forty years—from the late-fifties recordings of Billy Lee Riley and Jerry Lee Lewis to his present role at Sam Phillips Recording, where he works as a producer, engineer, guitarist, and handles publishing. Admittedly shy and generally reluctant to talk much about the old Sun days, Janes will say he doesn't put a lot of stock in complaints such as Gordon's.

. . . . *R O L A N D   J A N E S* . . . .

I was talking to one of those guys a while back and I'm not going to mention any names, but I happen to know that that person got paid because I saw it. I was there. And they said, "Well, I don't remember it," and I said, "Maybe you don't remember it, but I do. You may not have gotten what you thought you had coming, but then again you didn't pay for the session, you didn't do this, you didn't do anything. You just came in and did your thing and then you got your royalties, what you had coming. It was acceptable to you then. It's only in later years that suddenly you're saying, 'I didn't get this.'"

Really I think what it is, is frustration coming out, because people thought they deserved hit records that maybe they didn't get. Maybe they *did* deserve it, but that's the way it goes, man. I think I deserve to be a billionaire, but I don't think I'll ever be one. I don't know all the particulars and I don't pretend to, and don't intend to say I do, but I do know that some people got paid who said they didn't. If they didn't, they should've said something.

Some people had happy results there and some people didn't have happy results. You just have to live with what life deals you and do the best you can and that's all there is to it. And I think everybody really feels that way but they do show some frustration at times.

It's not entirely accurate to say that Sam Phillips lost his passion or professional interest in the blues. Following Presley's first two singles were Sun releases by Doctor Ross, Billy "The Kid" Emerson, and the Sammy Lewis–Willie Johnson Combo, and Phillips continued to record Rosco Gordon as late as 1958. The emphasis at the label did shift, however, as more and more white Southern firebrands heard themselves in Presley and arrived at Sun. But if the blues artists at the label were then for the most part abandoned, so too were the straight honky-tonkers who recorded for Phillips at roughly the same time.

Sun was never much of a country label, despite the crossover hits by Johnny Cash and Jerry Lee Lewis (who both really transcended the definition of country, anyway). But Sam Phillips did spend a little time experimenting with some of the outfits that played the honky-tonks and barn dances in and around Memphis. The label's first country single arrived in September 1953 with "Blues Waltz," the debut offering by the Ripley Cotton Choppers, and was followed five months later with efforts by Earl Peterson ("Boogie Blues") and Howard Serrat ("Troublesome Waters"), both trailed in May with maiden releases by Hardrock Gunter ("Gonna Dance All Night") and Doug Poindexter's Starlite Wranglers ("No She Cares No More for Me"). There were also fine sides, some of them unreleased, by the Dixieland Drifters, Mississippi Slim, and Bill Taylor and Smokey Joe.

Energetic and charmingly rough as they may have been, few of these singles proved much competition to the superior stuff then coming out of Nashville. Fittingly, Phillips's greatest country recordings came not from the traditional honky-tonkers in the mid-South, but through his brief association with Harmonica Frank Floyd, an itinerant songster with a singular style who fused the raw musical textures of Delta blues and the word-drunk concoctions of Woody Guthrie. Both "Swamp Root" (recorded by Phillips and licensed to Chess in 1951) and "The Great Medical Menagerist" (issued on Sun in 1954, less than a month before the release of Elvis's debut) make it clear that Phillips was looking for someone who could twist the blues and country-and-western into something new.

That someone wasn't Malcolm Yelvington, a country singer born just outside of Memphis in Covington, Tennessee, who had the misfortune of having his first Sun release just after the first two earth-shattering singles by Elvis. Yelvington's

brand of honky-tonk wasn't obsolete when his cover of Stick McGhee's "Drinkin' Wine Spo-Dee-O-Dee" was issued as Sun No. 211 in 1954, but, following the innovations Elvis introduced, it was about to undergo a major overhaul. On his later sessions at Sun you can hear Yelvington trying to adapt, often to good effect ("Trumpet," "It's Me Baby"). But both Phillips and Yelvington knew he could never completely make the transition from pure country to the hot-wired hybrid called rockabilly.

. . . M A L C O L M   Y E L V I N G T O N . . .

I grew up in Covington, Tennessee, which is about thirty-five miles north of Memphis. I was born and raised there and lived there until I was thirty-five, then I moved to Memphis. Before that I used to drive back and forth from Covington to Memphis, because I had a job there as a welder. I started to work for them in September 1951 and moved to Memphis in November of '53. Before I got into welding, I worked for a contractor in Covington. I laid brick, laid concrete, did electrical work. I guess I was what you'd call a jack-of-all-trades and master of none.

I was playing in bands all the time I was working. I started playing for the public during World War II. I was about twenty-two or twenty-three at that time. There were three theaters in Covington and one of them, the Gem Theater, was run by a man named Cliff Peck. I was up there doing some electrical work for them one day and he was telling me about fixing to start some amateur music on Saturdays in between the features and the movies. I told him I played guitar and sang a little bit, so he asked if I wanted to be on his show. I said yeah, as long as I could get off work long enough to do it. He didn't really audition anybody. If they came in and said they could play, he'd say, "Come on," because it was all amateur at that time anyway. So that first Saturday I went up there, and it was myself and one other guy by the name of Neil Hardin. He was a great fan of Ernest Tubb. Everything he sang was by Ernest

Memphis honky-tonker Malcolm Yelvington was always too country for Sam Phillips's roster of red-hot rockabillies. (Center for Southern Folklore Archives)

Tubb. I sang a variety of stuff, songs I picked up. The first song I sang on that stage was called "The One Rose." I had learned that song from a guy that had a radio show in Memphis on WMC—a guy named Gene Steel. "The Singing Salesman," they called him. I was scared to death on that stage. I had never been up in front of a crowd of people in my life, and back in those days on Saturday mornings those theaters were crammed. I mean they were full.

As the shows went along, a lot of other people started coming in to sing. A guy and his wife and his friend came up and they started singing on it. I had heard of him but had never met him until he came on the show. During the thirties he and the guy with him recorded for RCA. They had some pretty big hits, just the two of them. Anyway, his wife was a *real* piano player, and they started to play on the show and gave us a little more background music. Then some other guys started to come in and play, and the first thing you know, by the time the amateur shows were over, we had put together a band. There was Reece, Raspers, another young man on there that played guitar like a dobro and wound up playing steel, Miles Red Winn, and there was a guy who came back from the war named William Byrd, he played fiddle. We got him and his friend, Arnold Sanders, who played upright bass. So we put all these people together and we called ourselves the Tennesseans. We started playing a few schoolhouses and auditoriums, but we found out we could make the most money playing roadhouses—honky-tonks, you know? We were making more money there than we ever could playing a show date. Back in those days it was twenty-five, maybe thirty cents a head at a show date, and you didn't make much money like that unless you had overflow crowds, which we didn't. The cover for a roadhouse back then, though, was two dollars a couple or a dollar a head stag, and most of the time they'd give us all the door.

So we started playing at one in 1950, a place just north of Covington. About this time, though, the Tennesseans had pretty much broken up and I had joined a band called the Star Rhythm Boys. Eventually Reece came along and played piano with us. His wife had taught him piano fairly well. He wasn't a real high-class piano player, but he could get by in road-houses and places like that. Then we had a steel guitar player by the name of Cary Busey. It was him, Jake Riles on bass, Gordon Mashburn, Reece, and myself. One Saturday night, at the Clover Club just north of Covington, Cary Busey said, "This is my last night. I'm moving out of town to take another job." So we asked Red if he would be interested in joining the band. He had a little sling-neck Sears and Roebuck steel he played. So that next Saturday night Red showed up and that was the band that we played with from 1950 to 1957.

We were doing a lot of different stuff, including some of our own things. Reece was our main songwriter; he had a whole bunch of songs written. But he was also working at this time for an amusement place up in Covington that took care of pin-ball machines and jukeboxes. So he had to come to Memphis every week and pick up new records for the jukeboxes—guys like Eddy Arnold, Red Foley. And he'd buy five extra copies of each record, which his company paid for, and he'd give us each one of them so we could pick out songs we wanted to learn. We'd each learn our parts and that's how we learned how to play songs.

In 1954 they opened a radio station in Covington, WKDL, and the mayor of Covington got in touch with us to see if we would play that Sunday afternoon for the dedication of the station. So we played two songs, a hymn and a slow country song, and after the show there was a disc jockey there who called himself Country Ken. He had a show every Sunday from three in the afternoon to three thirty. So after the dedication he said, "Hey, Malcolm, how would y'all like to play this spot during my show?" I looked around at all the guys and they all said, "Yeah, let's do it." He asked if we had a program, and I said, "Nah, but we'll *get* one." So we all jumped in the car, went by a filling station and got two six-packs of beer, took off out in the country, found a little old dirt road and set there and drank beer and wrote out the program we were going to do that afternoon.

We started off with "Steel Guitar Rag," and Ken pointed to me and I stepped up to the mike and I said something like, "This is Malcolm Yelvington and the Star Rhythm Boys," and after a couple of numbers the bass player sang one, I sang for a bit, Reece did one, and that was it. We got through that first Sunday and it was a piece of cake from there on out. We played there for a year and a half every Sunday. In fact, there was so much demand for us that they wanted us on six days a week, plus the live show on Sunday. But we were all working full-time jobs, so after we'd do our Sunday show they'd tape us doing five fifteen-minute shows, and every day of the week they'd play that tape.

Eventually, Reece wanted to bring in some female singers. But since none of the rest of us wanted them, Reece left the band and I got Frank Tolley to come in. Then Gordon pulled out, and that just left Jake, Red, Frank, and myself. We got a fiddle player and we quit playing the Clover Club to play a club up on 64 Highway that was known as the Shadowlawn. That's where we were playing when we actually got our first record out.

Before I went to work for Sam, though, Reece went in to Memphis to pick up records, and there was a shop downtown called Home of the Blues. Reece knew the people that worked there pretty well. We had recorded three or four songs on a tape, just a little home-recorder thing, and he brought the tape down to Home of the Blues and told the guy there that anyone who came through—like a fella from a record company—get them to listen to it and see if they like it. So one day a guy from RCA named Ed Kazak came through and listened to it, and he liked it. Said, "I like that voice I'm hearing on there," which happened to be me, so Kazak gave his number in New York to the guy at the store—Murray Hill something-or-other—and said for me to call him collect.

So this guy called me at the welding shop and gave me Kazak's name and number, and I called him immediately and the guy offered me a contract. Said, "I'll put a contract in the mail this afternoon if you want to sign it." I said, "Well, how about the band?" He said, "Mr. Yelvington, I'm not interested in the band, I'm interested in you." He said RCA had musicians running out the ears—good ones, like Chet Atkins. All kinds of good musicians. And that's when I made the biggest mistake of my life, as far as music was concerned. I told him, "Well sir, if you're not interested in my band, you're not interested in me." And that was the last I heard of him.

See, I really liked the guys in the band, and we were all close friends and everything, and I really thought that me and the band were going to go places sooner or later. But after that happened, that's when I started going down to Sam's.

We had heard about this record company up in Memphis that was called Sun Records. They'd put out a record on a band from Ripley called the Ripley Cotton Choppers, and someone told us we should go see Sam. This was in 1953. So I went down to see him. Marion Keisker, Sam's secretary, was out front, and she sent me back to see Sam. He was back there by himself and I introduced myself to him. I said, "I understand you're putting records out." He said, "Yeah, a few." At that time it was mostly blues artists—Rufus Thomas, B. B. King, people like that. But Sam asked what we did and I said, "Well, we got what I think is a real good country band," but Sam said he wasn't really interested in country. I said, "Well, what are you interested in?" He said, "I don't know. I don't know really until I hear it." But I eventually talked him into listening to us, and we went in, in late '53, around December, and we were in the studio about eight hours that first day, recording mostly Reece's stuff.

We recorded one song called "Yakety Yak"—not that Coasters song—that Sam never did release, and we ran through a lot of stuff and none of it suited him. He said it was too country, or that it just wasn't what he was looking for. On into 1954 we kept going in, doing this and doing that, and one day I walked in there and he said, "Hey, Malcolm, remember I told you I wouldn't know what I was looking for until I heard it? Well, I heard it." He said it was a young man named Elvis Presley. He said, "We've been working on some stuff and I think it's going to be a hit for me." I said, "What's he like?" and Sam said he was a young man, about nineteen years old or so, been out of high school about a year. I thought to myself, "Boy, that's a long way from where I am." I'm thirty-five at this time, you know? I got a *daughter* in high school!

So Sam came out with Elvis's first two records. But in the meantime we went back in to work on some stuff, maybe in July or August, and he didn't like any of it. So I looked over at Gordon Mashburn, my lead guitar man, and said "Joe"—for some reason I always called him Joe—"kick off that 'Drinkin' Wine Spo-Dee-O-Dee,'" something we'd been playing in the honky-tonks for a long time. So he kicked it off and I started singing it, and we were doing it real up-tempo, and Sam looked up for a second, came out of the engineer room, and said, "Hold it, what's that you're doing? Play a little bit more of it." So we started playing and he moved around a couple of mikes and Sam said, "Let's cut that." And Reece had this country song called "Just Rollin' Along" that Sam kind of liked. It wasn't what he was looking for, but at least it was something to put on the other side of "Drinkin' Wine." I thought we had some other stuff that would've been better, but that's what Sam wanted. And what Sam wanted was what Sam got!

Anyway, that record came out. Marion had called me at work one day to ask if I'd heard the record. I said, "What record?" She said Dewey Phillips had been playing "Drinkin'

Wine" on his "Red Hot and Blue" show. I had no idea of that, but that afternoon when I got home from work, I cleaned up and made a beeline down there and got a few of the records. It felt so great to have a record out. You just knew you were going to be a star right off the bat, you know? You're going to be a big success, which is far from true, of course.

I had signed a contract with Sam that said I was supposed to have two or three releases in the first year. Well, it didn't come about that way. We had a lot of stuff recorded down there but none of it came out. It just wasn't what Sam was looking for. So in 1955, while I was still under contract to Sam, there was another company that come into Memphis and put up a studio out on Chelsea Avenue called Meteor Records. I had passed by there one day and saw the sign and went in there and talked to his guy, Les Bihari. I told him I had a band and he got interested right quick. Said, "Bring 'em on in," so we went in. This was after Reece and Gordon had left the group in 1955, so I had Frank Tolley on piano, Red on the steel, Jake on the bass, and me on rhythm guitar. So we played a bit and Bihari liked what he heard. We cut "Yakety Yak" and one called "A Gal Named Joe," both up-tempo. He released it in '55. I had it out under the name Mac Sales. I didn't really change my name, really, just shortened Malcolm and used my middle name, Sales. So it came out and I understand it did quite well, but I never collected a dime on it. I thought "Drinkin' Wine" did pretty good too, but I only got one royalty check the whole time I was there—a check for $48.

In 1956 I went back to Sam with a song I wrote called "Rockin' With My Baby." It's the only song I ever wrote in my life, and I tell people, "Well, at least I got one distinction: I wrote one song in my life and got it recorded and released on the Sun record label." Reece also had a song called "It's Me, Baby" so we put both of those on a demo tape one Sunday morning and I carried it down for Sam to listen to, and he liked it. He set up a date for us to come in and record, and that was the first time we had drums. It was recorded in June or July of 1956, and that was the last record I had released on Sun.

I recorded a lot more songs there after "Rockin' With My Baby." Most of it was recorded with Sam's staff band, because by that time most of my own band had gone off in their own directions. It was Roland Janes and James Van Eaton mostly. We did "Mr. Blues," and another one called "Trumpet." It was real up-tempo. There was "Blues in the Bottom of My Shoes." I don't know how many songs we had in the can, but Sam never released any of them.

As much stuff as I played for Sam, I was running out of material, and I didn't have no way of getting any more because Reece wasn't playing with us any longer. In fact, Reece died in November of 1958. I knew I wanted another chance. I wanted to get something out. I still had hopes. But I knew within all reason that I wasn't going to do anything like Elvis was doing. He was a young man, he was good-looking, he had that tremendous voice. Man, I loved that voice. So I knew that I wasn't ever going to make a big hit. When the band completely broke up, I joined the church and quit singing in the honkytonks. I quit singing and playing for the public for thirty years. Just quit.

In 1954, Sam Phillips brought Quinton Claunch and Bill Cantrell on board to ferret out new talent and expand the label's country roster. Claunch and Cantrell, country-gospel artists who toured the South together as the successful Blue Seal Pals, had initially approached Phillips in 1954 with a ballad titled "Daydreamin'," which they cut on a local singer named Bud Deckelman. Phillips passed on the recording, and the pair had Deckelman recut it for Meteor. The song didn't break nationally, but it sold well enough regionally to turn Phillips's ears red with rage. Rather than wait for the same thing to happen again, Phillips decided to forge an alliance. Claunch was soon making cameos on the first sessions of Carl Perkins and producing the initial recordings of the Miller Sisters and, most notably, Charlie Feathers.

A hot-tempered eccentric with an odd, pinched voice that could swing from a high tenor to a growling baritone, Feathers cut some terrific country sides under Claunch's direction, as well as co-writing the flip side of Sun No. 223 (Elvis's "I Forgot to Remember to Forget"), before knocking out definitive rockabilly classics such as "One Hand Loose" and "Bottle to the Baby" for the King label in Cincinnati. And somewhere along the way, Feathers decided that it was he—not Elvis, not Sam Phillips, not anyone else—who created rockabilly.

. . . . . . QUINTON CLAUNCH . . . . . .

I met Sam around 1942 at radio station WLAY in Muscle Shoals. He was doing some bookings for a gospel quartet out of Nashville, the John Daniel Quartet, and I showed up at some of those functions and we met there. He wasn't around Muscle Shoals very long after we met. He went to school down in Alabama, studying electronics and doing the radio bit. I went to work at Reynolds Metal Company in the area, and I got acquainted with another guy by the name of Edgar Clayton, who worked there also, and we started playing some shows— little get-togethers in that part of the world. Then we got us a radio show on the station where Sam had worked, WLAY, on Saturdays. Edgar and I worked at the station for a while, then we came to Memphis one time, just kind of nosing around to see what was going on, all that kind of good stuff, and at that point in time there was a real popular band in town, Slim Rhodes, and we met this guy, Bill Cantrell, after one of Rhodes's noontime shows. Come to find out he was from Alabama too, so we hit it right off and he decided to go back home with us. So we went back to Alabama and got another guy in the area, a bass player by the name of Dexter Johnson, and we started playing at the radio station over in Florence, WJOI. The program became fairly popular, I guess, because we were approached by a flour manufacturer out of Columbia,

Tennessee—Columbia Mill and Elevator Company, the makers of Blue Seal flour. They wanted to sponsor our program, and naturally we were looking for anything at that time. It became real popular and they kept adding stations and it got to be a fifteen-station network up through Alabama, Tennessee, and Mississippi. We were playing all over advertising that flour, and one day we got a call from the owner of the company wanting to know if we wanted to go over to WSM in Nashville. So that really excited us. That happened about 1945, maybe 1946, and we started getting bookings out of there through an agency that the flour company used for their commercials.

That was going pretty good and one day I got a call from down in Sheffield, from a comedian there named Rod Brasfield. He was on an NBC network show on WSM every Saturday night. He approached us to front him out on the road, so we traveled all over, man—Tennessee, Kentucky, Alabama, Mississippi, you name it. That went on for about a year, then one or two of the guys began to get tired. Bill quit and went to Chicago, and then I quit and moved to Memphis. At that point, I was married and my wife's parents lived in Jonesboro, Arkansas, and Memphis seemed like a halfway point between Muscle Shoals and Jonesboro. I got a regular job with a supply company and went on working for them for forty-three and a half years, but kept doing my music on the side. And Bill had moved to Memphis when he found out I was there.

By the time I came to Memphis, Sam had started this little recording studio, and knowing Sam, I went in and got reacquainted with him, because Bill and I had found this country singer named Bud Deckelman who was absolutely great. He could've gone as far as anyone up in Nashville. But Bill and I had written this song called "Daydreamin'," and we went into a little recording studio here in town, at Poplar at Crosstown, to do a demo, and we took it by Sam's. He said, "Well, I like the concept but you need to do this and do that." But I felt like I knew as much about country music as he did, so we went back home to think about what we were going to do. We decided to go over to another studio, Meteor, run by Les Bihari, and that song flipped him out. He wanted to get us together and do it right away. So naturally we did that and he put it out on Meteor Records and that thing was number one in Memphis, Cleveland, Ohio, New Orleans, and Des Moines, Iowa. And when that thing hit, it just set Sam on fire. He couldn't stand it. It just shocked the living hell out of him. So he called us in and wanted Bill and me to be talent scouts for Sun Records. He had already signed up one guy, Charlie Feathers, so he called us in to work with him.

I liked Charlie's voice, but he didn't have an education, and I wondered how far it would go. Charlie was a little bit self-centered, to say the least. He was his own worst enemy, to tell the truth. He didn't trust anybody. But we were able to work with him and come up with three or four records there—"I've Been Deceived," "Defrost Your Heart," "Wedding Gown of White." If that guy had just had a little education and a little common sense, he could've gone farther than any of those guys. He could've been where Carl Perkins had got, or a lot of those guys. He could feel a song, but, man, putting up with him was something else. It was insecurity. He's got it in his mind that he created rockabilly. He taught Elvis how to sing, to hear him tell it. He didn't do anything, aside from writing that song with Stan Kesler that Elvis recorded, and he was there on occasions when Elvis was recording. He might've been on speaking terms back before Elvis got big, when he was getting started. I don't know. I guess he resented that Elvis came in there and started doing some things that maybe he had in mind to do himself. He just couldn't handle it.

Bill and I were cutting pretty much straight country, but Memphis could never cut down-home redneck country. They didn't have the engineers that understood that music, didn't have the musicians who could play it professional like those guys in Nashville. We were cutting country, but it wasn't in the same mold as Nashville. It was a lot more rough. Carl Perkins had this one song, "Let the Jukebox Keep on Playing," that I played that peck rhythm on—a thump rhythm on guitar that Sam asked me to do. It went real well. I knew Carl had something on the ball. That feel he had. And Ray Harris had kept bugging Sam, and Sam kind of liked what he heard in him, so he told him to work on some things and bring them by. So we'd go out to Ray's house and just work, work, work, work, and came up with that "Greenback Dollar." We went back to Sam and he said, "Yeah, come on." Ray put his heart and soul into everything he did.

The Harris record was released in 1956, not long before Claunch and Cantrell left the label. There was a dispute over Phillips removing one of their songs ("Sure to Fall") from a Carl Perkins single, and besides, Claunch never shared Phillips's interest in rockabilly.

. . . . *CLAUNCH* . . . .

Sun was getting kind of played out there after a while. Sam wasn't doing exactly what he said he was going to do. He was getting more into that rock and roll stuff and these guys were coming in with their own bands, so the session work kind of dried up. Sam wanted us to work with Barbara Pittman, but she never did anything big. She couldn't sing. Everybody knew she didn't have the voice. We worked with her night after night, month after month, and couldn't get nothing going, so we gave up. She was pretty young, didn't have the voice, no range. Just couldn't put anything into song. Sam's got a pretty good ear, but I can't imagine he thought she had any talent along that line.

Elvis was going to cut one of my songs one time, called "The Voice of a Fool," back in 1956, 1957. Barbara Pittman did the demo on it and I had gotten home from work one day and Elvis had called wanting to know if I could come out to his house, to Graceland. He already had the demo and he wanted me to come down and discuss the song. I was kind of thrilled to get that call. He said, "Man, I'm gonna do your song." I said, "Man, have at it." Then he got called to the army and it got lost in the shuffle. That was the last of that.

So Bill and I left Sun and went on to work with another record label, O.J. Records. We had Red Matthews and we cut some things on Brother Dave Gardner. Then I started Hi with Ray and Joe Cuoghi.

Hi debuted in 1957 with a rockabilly single by Carl McVoy, one of Jerry Lee Lewis's cousins. The label floundered for nearly two years, and Claunch had departed before Hi landed its first hit, the Bill Black Combo's "Smokie, Part 2" from 1959. In the mid-sixties Claunch founded Goldwax, which enjoyed modest success, most notably with Southern soul singer James Carr.

THREE

Goin' to the Rockhouse

If Phillips's increased attention to rockabilly sent numerous blues and country artists into exile, or at least to other labels, it opened the studio and label to a new breed of Southern rockers—ones who, like Elvis, listened as closely to rural country blues as the honky-tonk being broadcast from the "Grand Ole Opry" and the "Louisiana Hayride." Men like Billy Lee Riley, Roland Janes, and Jack Clement, who arrived at the studio together after Clement took a recording he'd made of Riley to Phillips for mastering.

Riley was one of Sun's wildest artists both in and out of the studio, a raw-voiced singer who at his best rocked like a dream fusion of Elvis Presley and Little Richard. Riley was also at the helm of Sun's staff band, along with drummer J. M. Van Eaton and guitarist Janes, a country-based picker from northeast Arkansas whose style would blossom into one of the most distinct and influential in rock and roll.

Clement, born in the unfortunately named Memphis suburb of Whitehaven and a journeyman country musician in his pre-Sun life, was a gifted songwriter, producer, and engineer who acted as Phillips's right-hand man and ad hoc producer after the boss began to lose interest in his enterprise. Together, Riley, Janes, and Clement were involved in the making of some of Sun's finest recordings, from Jerry Lee Lewis's "Great Balls of Fire" to Riley's own "Flying Saucer Rock and Roll."

. . . . . B I L L Y L E E R I L E Y . . . .

I was born in Pocahontas, Arkansas, in 1933. When I was three we moved to Osceola, which was maybe a hundred miles west of Pocahontas, and that's where I spent most of my childhood days. We left there in about 1942 and moved back to Pocahontas for a bit, then we moved to Lake City, Arkansas, where for the first time we had a sharecropper on the farm. We lived there for three years, then we moved to Forrest City, where we spent a year farming as sharecroppers on a plantation. That's where I really started playing blues.

I got started at a very early age doing blues, playing with the black people at the plantations, on the front porches, and under shade trees. Most of the time I just watched. But there were a few people there that taught me how to play.

Living on a plantation, you have to make all the entertainment around. I rarely went to town; nobody had a car, there was nothing to do. Once in a while, a tent show would come through town, the old medicine-man show. I'd been to a lot of them. They would come to town and set up a tent and they'd have music, and most of it was hillbilly music, mountain music. They'd sell all types of things—they would sell pictures and candy and medicine, all kinds of weird things. But it was about the only entertainment we had unless we made our own. We'd work in the fields from about sunup until sundown for five days a week, and on the weekends what are you going to do? You don't have theaters out there. There were practically no cars to get into town.

There was one fella that lived on the plantation, a black fella, and he was the only one out there that I remember of all the black guys that had a car. The landowner had sold him an old '35 Ford and charged him ten times what it was worth. I'd say he's still paying on that car. But he had a little business going on where he would carry people into town. A round trip cost thirty-five cents, and he'd load that ol' car up so he was making ten or fifteen bucks a weekend and that was more than he was making most of the year as a farmer.

Maybe once a month we would get into town and do shopping. I used to go up there and just walk around. There was a lot of gambling going on, and we'd always be sneaking into this place. The plantations would have a big store, a general store, where everybody trades. But they also had a little recreation house for the adults where the black guys would play cards and gamble and drink in there. And we'd sneak in there every once in a while and they always had a little music going and we go in there and watch them gamble and fight and whatever. We'd always get run out.

We also had baseball teams, where this farm would play that farm. We'd all get into an old wagon and ride over to the next farm, which would be ten or twelve miles away. It was always on a Sunday, and they'd always have concessions. Somebody would be barbecuing something. To us it was all great, but the music was better than any of it.

The first music I loved was country. Remember, in those days country was different. There was a lot of blues in it. I heard people like Jimmie Rodgers, who to me was always blues. There was a lot of that to his music. You didn't hear the black music on the radio, but there was something about it. Something about how it would tell a story that the other music wasn't telling. I think it was me relating it to how we were all living out there—how poor people lived out there. That's what pulled me into it.

My dad had given me my first harmonica when I was six years old, and by the time we moved to Forrest City I had heard all these harmonica players and I learned to play the blues on it. I was also playing a bit of guitar. But the blues was just a part of me, and it's been a part of me ever since. It shows in all the music I do. If I sing country, I've still got my blues in there. It's a part of me. I think it was just a natural expression of the shape we were in, and we could relate to it better than we could all those "Oh My Darlin'," "Look at the Sunshine" kind of songs. I think when we heard a song about how mean the bossman is and how poor I am and how hungry I am, and this man run out with this man's wife, you know, it meant something because we lived that and saw that. We didn't see that other side. We didn't know what was going on over on the other side of the world, or on the other side of the *fence* even!

Carl Perkins once made the statement, "We didn't know we was poor till we started school." Well, we *knew* we was poor. We just didn't know how the other people were living. We knew we didn't have anything and our neighbors didn't have anything. But we had nothing to be ashamed of. We just enjoyed life, and I think we enjoyed life more than the people who had the money and worried about keeping it. We didn't have to worry about keeping it. We didn't have it!

When I first got to Forrest City, there was a kid there named Tommy Hamblin, his whole family were musicians, and he and I became friends. We were the same age, and I found out a bit later that he had a little ol' Stella guitar and he could play his blues on it. He played a lot of country, too, and his dad played mandolin and his brother played guitar, and when he found out I had a guitar, of course he and I spent a lot of time together. He was teaching me things, but I was mostly taught by the people out on the farm.

I didn't actually play in a band until I went in the army in 1949, at the age of fifteen. I won some talent contest at the post in Seattle, Washington, and that got me really interested in playing music, but I was playing country. I got out of the service in '53 and the first thing I did when I got out was form a country band. I got us some radio shows. We were actually played on two radio shows simultaneously. We'd record on Sunday and those would be played every day on both of these stations, one in Paragul and one in Jonesboro, where I was living at the time. Paragul was like eighteen miles away and we'd go up there on Sundays and we'd record shows for the whole week, and we'd come back to Jonesboro to record a week's worth of shows in Jonesboro. And at the same time, my bass player and his wife and I would get up about five o'clock in the morning and do a live gospel show on another station in Jonesboro before I'd go to work. I was working at that time in a shoe factory. So I played a lot. We did high school dances, a few clubs, but it wasn't nothing really big until I went to Memphis and got this contract at Sun Records.

I didn't come to Memphis for music, though. My brother-in-law lived there and he had been wanting to open a restaurant. He asked me if I would be interested in investing in a restaurant and I thought about it for a while and we decided to go out looking for one. We went to Kentucky first and were going to buy an old railroad cafe up there in Paducah. We looked at it and we weren't too happy with what we saw so we went back to Memphis and bought a place on Poplar Avenue, not too far from Sun. So not knowing anything about the location or the restaurant business in general, we just bought a place and opened it up. We sold beer and sold good food, too, but we found out that the place was just a joint—had always been just an old dive. But we kept it for four or five months, until we got closed by the city because of a gunfight in there one night.

So we lost all that. I was living in Memphis doing whatever I could. My brother-in-law was a meat cutter, so he got me some jobs doing that. But I was in Jonesboro visiting my wife's folks one Christmas in 1955. My folks lived in Nettleton, which was about three or four miles away, and I was going to go after that Christmas to my mother's house. Along the way I saw two guys on the road hitchhiking, so I picked them up and said,

"I'm only going three or four miles, but I'll take you up to the highway where you'll have a better chance of catching a ride." Come to find out, it was Jack Clement and Slim Wallace. That was the first time I'd ever met these guys.

We got to talking about music, and they were playing at a club in Paragul that Slim Wallace owned. I told them I was a singer, a country singer, and before we quit talking I had brought them all the way to Memphis. I didn't even go to my mother's house. I had brought them all the way to their house—Slim Wallace lived on Fernwood and they were building a studio in the garage. So we got to talking about that and they took me out there and showed me what they were doing and asked me if I'd like to maybe work some in their band. And I said, "Yeah." It paid about ten, twelve bucks for a Saturday night. So after they got the studio finished Slim and Jack asked me if I wanted to come in and record. I was supposedly going to be the first artist on Fernwood Records.

. . . . *JACK CLEMENT* . . . .
I had been going to college for about two and a half years in Memphis, after I got out of the service. I had had enough of that, so I went to work at a building supply place for a few months, and I wasn't liking that much. But during that time I produced a record with Billy Lee Riley. We cut it at a radio station in Memphis, WMPS. It was going to come out on Fernwood, a label I was going to start with Slim Wallace, who had put up the money to pay for the thing and had built a studio in his garage. We hadn't finished the studio yet, but we practiced out there and got it ready to record, and then went down to WMPS for two or three hours and made this record. It had two slapping basses on it. I figured if one slapping bass was good, two would be better. It was neat.

I took the master tape to Sam to put it on a little acetate master for us so we could press it up. That was the only reliable place that did it. He had the best setup in town. It was pretty antiquated, actually, but it was the best thing in Memphis. So I went there and left the tapes with him and went back the next week to pick them up and he said he wanted to talk to me. We went back in the control room and he said he really liked the record and wanted to know if I'd be interested in having him put it out on Sun. I talked to my partner, Slim. We didn't really have the money to do all that stuff, so it was better that way.

After Sam and I talked about that he asked me what I was doing and I said I was out here working at Clark and Fay, that I had been doing that a couple months but didn't really like it that much. He said, "Maybe you ought to come to work here." So he offered me a job and a couple weeks later I went to work there.

See, Sam had been doing it all and he was kind of burned out on the whole deal. He wanted to get it to where he'd have an assistant. He'd tried some people, but he liked the way that first record sounded that I had brought in. He said, "This is the first rock and roll anybody's brought in here." He liked that sound. But it was his sound. I just went and did his sound, except I had the two basses. Basically he'd bought something I had done, and there wasn't any changes he had to make to it. It wasn't like we were going to overdub or remix it or nothing. What you heard was what you got.

I just worked there, although, you know I did go in there as a producer. I had produced something on my own and he liked it and bought it. But I was a trainee at the same time. I didn't know much about operating the equipment at that point, but I was dying to get my hands on it. That was what I was really into. I was just in there doing something all the time. I'd bring people in and experiment with different things because I was having a ball playing with all that equipment and that echo. I finally had my hands on echo!

I was born in northeast Arkansas, in a little community called Brookings, on August 20, 1933. According to my arithmetic that makes me thirty-two years old. I was raised between there and St. Louis, back and forth over several different trips. My parents were divorced and my mother moved there to find work and support us. The kids were left with her. I lived there with her and my father stayed in this part of the country. I had three brothers and three sisters. I'm next to the youngest. I had cousins and uncles that were musical and my father was musical, although I never heard him play but a couple of times. I had a couple of brothers and sisters who were musical, so it was kind of in my family. One picked it up from the other. My first instrument was a mandolin. I tried to buy one through the Sears and Roebuck catalog and that wasn't available. They sold them but they didn't have this particular model, so I ended up buying a used guitar and started from that. I had an uncle that had a band, Pop and the Midnight Ramblers, a country band.

Basically I just played rhythm guitar and sang, then started playing lead solo parts. On down the road I finally determined—or maybe it was determined for me—that I should stick to the guitar and leave the singing to somebody else. I was probably all right, but I was a little too shy to be a star, so to speak, but I could play the guitar and hide behind everybody else. I've written a few songs. Actually I've written quite a few. I never really actively tried to get too many of mine recorded, although I've had maybe a couple of dozen recorded over the years. In the beginning I didn't write songs. I never really considered myself a songwriter. I just wrote a few songs and happened to get a few of them recorded, but I didn't begin as a songwriter.

In my young years I played with my uncle's band, but growing up in St. Louis there really weren't that many bands playing the kind of music that I played. And I was a little young, too.

67

Guitar great Roland Janes looking drop-dead cool in the mid-fifties. "I was a little too shy to be a star, but I could play guitar and hide behind everybody else." (Center for Southern Folklore Archives)

When I first started playing I was about twelve. While I was in the Marine Corps I played with some bands, and when I came out I played with a couple of bands and I got into the recording thing. I went into the Marine Corps in 1953. It was during the

Korean thing and you were going to go in one way or the other, and I'd seen a couple of John Wayne movies, I guess. I was only in a couple years. I went in as an active reserve and came out as a ready reserve. I had moved to Memphis just shortly before I enlisted for some reason. I can't tell you why because I don't know. I enlisted in St. Louis but was living in Memphis at the time. I'd only been here a few months and I knew I was going to get drafted pretty soon anyways, so I decided to go ahead and get it over with. I drove back to St. Louis and enlisted there.

When I got out of the Marine Corps is when I got active in music. I'd always wanted to be a musician. I had gotten in a couple of bands and there was some recording happening in Memphis and there wasn't any recording in St Louis. I just struggled with a couple of guys. I actually ran across Jack Clement, who was a songwriter and musician, and he was trying to cut a couple of records. One was on an artist named Billy Lee Riley. He asked me if I would help him cut the record and I said, "Sure, I'd be glad to. I'd love it." From that, after we got it cut he came to Sun Records and Sam Phillips, and Sam heard what we did and he liked it and signed Billy to a contract and hired Jack to be his engineer. Jack kind of brought me in as a house guitar player.

The way I met Jack, there was a guy here in town named J. P. "Doc" McQueen, and he was an accountant for Union Planters Bank. Doc had a little old two-tape-recorder setup in his home. He was a songwriter, an amateur songwriter. He loved musicians; all the musicians used to hang around at his house. Doc had run an ad in the paper looking for musicians to help him cut some demos on some songs that he wrote. I answered the ad and I met Doc, and by hanging around his house there we got to be real good friends and I met all the other musicians that were hanging around there at the time. Chips Moman hung around there a little later than that, the Burnette boys, a bunch of people. There was a fellow named Kenneth Herman, a steel guitar player in town. We got to be pretty good buddies and ran around a lot together and he told me about Jack Clement, said that Jack Clement and Slim Wallace were building a studio in Slim's garage and trying to cut some records and he wanted to know if I'd like to go out and meet them. I said, "I'd love to." That's how I met Jack and Slim.

"Trouble Bound" was the first record I worked on. We recorded the first side, "Rock With Me Baby," at WMPS radio station, and we recorded a country song called "Think Before You Go"—I don't think it was ever released—at the radio station also. But Sam wanted something a little more rocking for the other side so we recorded "Trouble Bound" at Sam's studio. There's some confusion on that due to what people had read on tape boxes, but that's the true story. I know because I was there.

There were two basses on "Rock With Me Baby"—Slim Wallace and the other guy was Jan Ledbetter. Slim was partners with Jack and he was a bass player, and Jack, for some reason or another, wanted Jan. Jan was an excellent upright bass player. But there were two upright bass players on that. It was unique at that time. One upright bass is hard enough to record technically and two was quite an accomplishment. We were a little tentative, you know, because we were scared to death probably, but I think it's a pretty good-sounding record. It's a good start. There's only four of us on "Trouble Bound"—Johnny Bernero played drums, I played guitar, and Billy played acoustic guitar, I guess, and I don't remember who played bass on that. It wasn't Billy.

I never dreamed that I'd play on a record. I was so thrilled to play on a record that—and I'm not a crying-type guy—the first time I heard ["Trouble Bound"] on the radio I actually had tears come to my eyes. I was that thrilled. It was a wonderful feeling at that time. I got a real thrill out of it. I think all of us did.

Jack had been in the Marine Corps also and was a songwriter and played with all kinds of people. He played with the Stoneman Family in Washington, D.C., because he was stationed there. He was in some kind of special services up there. He had written a lot of songs. Jack was an excellent singer and songwriter and an excellent producer as well as an engineer. A very talented man. He never spoke up for himself much but I think he's extremely talented. Sam recognized that talent and hired Jack, and, of course, he was a big influence on Jack. Jack learned a lot from Sam. He learned an awful lot from Sam.

In the beginning Jack's main function was to try and discover new talent, but when they got down to cutting records—the Johnny Cashes and people like that—Sam came back into the picture. But Jack eventually wrote several songs for Johnny and was real effective. He was a very talented man. Sam, as successful as he was, he was very busy and he was getting to where he couldn't handle all of the things he had to handle and he really needed someone. He chose Jack, and I thought that spoke very well of Jack. And I feel proud that Jack chose me. It might have been a matter of convenience. I don't know; I never asked him.

It was a job as such. I was just on call when they needed to do a session. They would call whoever they wanted to use and I turned out to be available most of the time, I guess. With Riley, we ended up with Jimmy Van Eaton playing drums in our band and also Jimmy Wilson, a piano player, maybe a year later, and our band basically did most of the sessions. A lot of the artists had their own bands and they would use their bands sometimes and sometimes maybe one of us or all of us were included in parts of their band. Not on every record.

Van Eaton was working with a guy and they had a good little rocking band, and Van Eaton really stood out. Everybody thought he was a really good drummer. We needed a drummer, so Billy and me decided to see if we could recruit him for

our band. So we actually went out to where they were play-
ing and talked with him, and he decided to join our band.
In joining our band he became part of the recording thing.
He was just a kid. When we did our first session with Jerry
Lee Lewis, Jack called me up and said, "Hey man, I got this
piano player guy down in Louisiana. He's pretty good,
man. I'm going to cut some tapes on him. Want to come
down and help us out?" I said, "Sure." He said, "You think
Van Eaton would do it?" I said, "I think he would." He said,
"Would you mind going by and picking him up?" because
he couldn't drive. So I went by his house and picked him
up. He was too young to have a driver's license yet. I got a
kick out of when they did that movie on Jerry a while back.
All the people playing us were thirty-five or so and we
were anywhere from eighteen to twenty-two, including
Jerry. I think he was twenty-one.

. . . . *R I L E Y* . . . .

I knew what was going on in Memphis because Elvis had
been on Sun Records. But as far as being on records, I was a
Hank Williams fan, and MGM stuck out in my mind. I
always said, "I'm going to be an artist for MGM, like Hank
Williams," which I never was. But I didn't know that much
about Sun Records. I didn't come to Sun, as a lot of people
said they did, to audition and all that. But by the time this
was happening with Fernwood, I'd been living in Memphis
a while and I learned enough to know that I would be happy
to be on Sun. I'd heard some of Elvis and I said, "Hey, I
could do that." And of course, Carl Perkins, I was a fan of
his for a long time. There was some kind of feel there that I
sort of related to. I was feeling stuff coming out of this studio, that I had felt before. I didn't know what it was, though.
To be honest with you, I was young and didn't know that
much about anything. But Sam liked what he heard, so he

made Jack a deal and made me a deal: I got an artist contract out of it, and Jack got a contract out of it as an engineer and a producer.

When Jack got his deal here, he did a great job. Sam and I didn't really get along per se. We respected each other, but we clashed. I think that I wanted to do one thing, and he knew what I wanted to do, but he wanted me to do another.

. . . . *CLEMENT* . . . .

Sam and I hit it off good. I always thought he was kind of a nut. I always thought he was full of shit. And he was. And still is. But that's part of it. I've come to appreciate him as a genius, actually. I think he was some kind of genius. He had some kind of thing. It's hard to define it, but he knew how to get people going. Just the way he reacted to things. There was something about him that made you want to perform for him, because when he liked something he *loved* it. And when he didn't like it, he *hated* it. And he hated most everything. But when he liked something, he loved it, so it was just a great pleasure to really knock him out.

. . . . *RILEY* . . . .

Jack Clement was a genius and still is. In my opinion, Jack was as much or more of a musical genius than Sam ever hoped to be. Sam only recorded two sides on me while I was here. Jack did everything else. Sam had done nothing as far as discovering me. Jack discovered me. Sam gets a lot of credit for discovering artists. He takes credit for discovering Jerry Lee Lewis, but Jerry Lee Lewis just walked in the studio one morning when I came in here, and he didn't know anybody. We introduced ourselves and I gave him a job working with me, working in my band. J. M. Van Eaton was the drummer, Roland Janes was the guitar player, Pat O'Neil was the bass player, replacing Marvin Pepper, who started with me. Martin Willis was my horn man. That's the group that played on 80 percent of everything that came out of Sun from 1957 to 1959, all of us together or parts of us. The piano player I hired after Jerry quit was Jimmy Wilson. And Jimmy Wilson played on sessions with everybody. J.M. was the first drummer Cash used. All Jerry's stuff, it was usually Roland, me, and J.M., and then J. W. Brown came to town and started playing bass. Before he came I would play bass or Roland would.

But that first session we did with Jerry Lee was truly accidental. Sam wasn't even here when that one happened. "Crazy Arms" was not planned. We was just out there jamming and it was released, and I happened to get the last note on guitar on it. The way it happened, Roland Janes and J.M. and Jerry Lee and I were in the studio just jamming. I think we were in here to do something for somebody else, because, like I said, we did all the sessions back then. When the song first started, it was only J.M. and Jerry Lee playing the song. Roland was in the john, and I was in the studio playing around on an upright bass, which I can't play at all. I wasn't playing on mike or anything. But Jerry and J.M. were doing their thing, and nobody knows Jack has the machines on. Nobody knows this. So Roland comes out of the john, comes into the studio at the same time that I put the bass down. He picks it up and starts trying to play it as I pick up his guitar. I sit down and about the time I'm ready to play, Jerry Lee's about done with the song and I hit that one chord— *thrrranng*—and that's the one they released. You hear all these stories that it was all planned and this and that, but that is the true story.

It was very frantic working with Jerry Lee. This isn't anything that everybody doesn't already know, but he had a big ego and he always thought that he was the best there ever was. And nobody ever takes that away from him. He was

The picture sleeve for Jerry Lee Lewis's 1958 single "High School Confidential." The song was better than the movie it accompanied.

talented. But he lost a lot of that talent by bragging on himself all the time, as far as I was concerned. He didn't need to brag. You could just watch him and know how good he was. But he was not easy to work with. Sometimes he just wanted Jerry Lee on the record, and if he didn't hear enough of him, he didn't like that. But a lot of times he would come in and a session would go real good. Then we'd come in here and sit all night and it would be nothing but total confusion.

I think Jerry Lee is probably the most misunderstood man in the world. Jerry Lee is Jerry Lee and all of us want to be taken for what we are, and he's what he is. Jerry Lee Lewis will give you the shirt off his back and is one of the greatest guys in the world. But at the same time he's got a little bit of a chip on his shoulder and he also won't take anything off of anybody. But he's one of the finest people in the world, man, and one of the greatest talents. Stop and think about it. A guy as great as Jerry Lee was, there were going to be a lot of people jealous of the man, because you could have a hundred piano players come in a room and they could be really good piano players, and Jerry Lee sits down at the piano and it's over with. All the piano players, and everybody will gather around Jerry Lee.

I worked on the road with Jerry for a long time and we had package shows where we had Chuck Berry, the Everly Brothers, Buddy Holly, you name it. Seventeen, eighteen, twenty acts on the show and all of them with hit records. After the show, they'd close the curtains and Jerry Lee would sit down at the piano and start playing and singing and all these stars would gather around him like they were teenage fans. That's how much talent the man had. But at the same time, there was some animosity toward him and some jealousy of him, but he wasn't like that.

On the road he was just strictly a showman, more or less. He did what the people wanted to hear. We'd had people close the shows on us several times because people thought he was too wild. But [the shows] were not like they are now. You can get away with anything now. But then if you wiggled your butt a little bit they wanted to close the curtain on you. He wasn't vulgar. He did a couple things that maybe he shouldn't have done, but I've seen other people do much worse. He was really very religious-oriented. It depended on the audience reaction and where we were at and the quality of the piano. He used to be given some pretty bad pianos to play. People didn't realize then how important the instrument was to him. A lot of the wild stuff he did on piano would be out of frustration because they'd give him pianos that maybe five or six of the notes didn't play. Back then we didn't make demands like you do these days—like the piano has to be a so-and-so with a certain sheen to the polish. Back then we didn't ask for anything. We just took what they gave us and he'd sometimes get kind of frustrated with it.

A lot of people think that he was jealous of Elvis. He wasn't jealous of Elvis. In his mind, he thought he was a much better performer than Elvis and who's to say that he wasn't? There's two different trains of thought. Elvis was a heartthrob type performer and Jerry Lee was a knock-down, drag-out, go-get-'em type of guy. They were both great in their own field. I would've loved to have seen them on the stage together. I think they would've had a ball. They were actually good friends. People don't know that. Elvis had a great amount of respect for Jerry Lee, and Jerry Lee had a great amount of respect for Elvis. Now, they could each do a song and it would sound totally different. With Jerry, we never did that many of Elvis's songs, and usually the ones we did we'd just take a couple of takes on them and go on to something else, but they approached the song from two totally different directions and from different perspectives. Elvis played instruments—he played guitar and played the rhythm on the piano—but he wasn't a musician like Jerry Lee. See, you have to look at Jerry Lee like this: The piano is an extension of Jerry Lee. It was part of him. What he sang and what he played was like a hand and a glove, and Elvis sang to what somebody else played, if you know what I mean. But they were both great in their own way. I think they had a tremendous amount of respect for each other.

People have never really seen Jerry Lee do all that he is capable of as a piano player. The man could play anything. He could play more with his left hand than most people could with their right hand. He can do equally well on both hands. A lot of those solos you're hearing on those piano things, the slow things, is half his right hand, half his left hand. People just can't do that, but he does. Jerry Lee was an original. He can take a song and he'll rewrite your song for you—not with a pencil and paper—and you'll end up with a better song than you had when you sat down with it. And he'll add some stuff on the piano that makes it great.

Although Jack Clement's production work on the early Jerry Lee Lewis sessions was spare and unfettered—mostly using just drums, bass, and minimal guitar—he'll be the first to tell you that he's always had a tendency to overproduce, a tendency that was never quite shared by Phillips. Still, Clement's work at Sun was amazingly diverse—from the bareboned rockers he cut with Jerry Lee, Billy Lee Riley, and Sonny Burgess to the more elaborate productions of hits by Johnny Cash, upon a few of which Clement poured extra guitars and vocal choruses

. . . . *CLEMENT* . . . .

I'm not sure exactly what the first record I did there was, but Roy Orbison was one of the first. I thought he and his band were kind of pissy at first. Roy always had these crazy ideas. He was ahead of what we could do there in Memphis, really. He was thinking orchestrations, choirs—big production stuff. He wanted production numbers, like he ultimately wound up doing. I told Roy he'd never make it as a ballad singer. He never let me forget that, either. I've been right a few times. Of course, I've been wrong a few times.

I cut some things with Sonny Burgess that I thought were pretty good. I probably worked harder with him than with anybody else and had less success with it. I think it had something to do with sex appeal, maybe, timing. Whatever. He was pretty much stuck over in Arkansas, and he never really did get out and tour that much. If he'd had more promotion, he could've done something, but Sam never really promoted stuff much. He'd just send out about 1,500 copies to radio stations and talk to some distributors and then he hired [brother] Jud Phillips to be his promotion man. But Jud didn't do much except go to New York and get Jerry Lee on TV shows, hang out with Dick Clark, pay people off. Stuff like that. But that's what he needed to do. There wasn't ever any heavy promotion, but they didn't need to. Everybody was waiting to hear that product, they were just sitting there waiting to get some new releases, and as soon as they got them they would listen to them. They may not play it, but they're at least going to listen to it. Some of them they played, some of them they didn't.

But me and Roy got to be big buddies. We hung out a lot, and I worked hard trying to cut something with him, but we never cut anything. Best thing we cut was that "Rockhouse" thing. "Sweet and Easy to Love," that was a good one. I guess we cut better stuff, but Sam kind of lost interest in him. Sam, he had a weakness: Whoever was his biggest selling artist was the one that seemed to get all the attention. That's the reason he loved Johnny Cash.

Gradually, Sam would turn more and more of these people over to me, and more and more he wouldn't come into the studio. He'd come in later, in the afternoon maybe. Like I said, he was kind of burned out on doing that stuff. I'm that way now. I can't hardly stand to go into the studio, unless it's something really, really intriguing. It's just the music that's in the world right now, and I'm not interested in making any of *that* crap. If I can't do something different, I don't want to get in the studio. And the older I get, the more particular I get. I've never tried to do something that I didn't like, because if I didn't like it, I didn't understand it. It wasn't that I might not have been willing, I just didn't know how to get that commercial. I've never tried to stay with the trends. I've always tried to ignore that. But the fact is, most of my hit records have been *not* trendy, you know?

*

Clement's records with Johnny Cash not only weren't trendy, they were unlikely hits from a label known for frantic, crazed rock and roll. A native Arkansan with a dark baritone not unlike Ernest Tubb's, Cash moved to Memphis in 1954 after a stint in the air force. His brother Roy introduced him to a pair of Memphis auto mechanics—guitarist Luther Perkins and bassist Marshall Grant—who played gospel on a Sunday radio program. After woodshedding for a while in Perkins's living room, the trio auditioned at Sun.

They were an odd bunch. Cash's big, booming voice had a tendency to go flat, and his musicians were hardly virtuosos. It was all Perkins could do to pick out skeletal single-string riffs, and Grant slapped out the time on his clickety-clack upright bass. The combination was like nothing else in country music and proved compelling enough to result in sixteen Top 40 hits on *Billboard*'s country-and-western chart and eleven singles on the magazine's pop chart, including "Guess Things Happen That Way," "Ballad of a Teenage Queen," and "Ways of a Woman in Love," among the most lavish productions in the Sun canon.

. . . . *CLEMENT* . . . .

At Sun, I took it in a whole new direction. With Johnny Cash, it started with adding a vocal group. Then we started adding other stuff to Cash's band, and the first thing was me. I played guitar on a whole lot of that stuff. On "Big River" I played the guitar and the bass drum at the same time. I had the guitar tuned up in some open key. I don't remember exactly which one, but it worked out. Also, I would think up a lot of those licks that Luther Perkins played. I would help him work a lot of that stuff out. Then we'd add piano. It just got a lot more orchestral when I came into the picture, because I've always sort of thought that way. I've been known to overproduce a lot of stuff.

It kind of started with "Ballad of a Teenage Queen." I had my guitar on it and the voices. That was one where I had Sam on the board because I had to play rhythm guitar on it, then we overdubbed the vocal group later. We overdubbed that group and it got kind of silly. We had them doing those *bah-doo-pah-doo*s on there and I liked it, so we kept it that way. Sam always hated "Teenage Queen." He still hates it. I got hits for him, but he hated some of them. Like "Teenage Queen." I didn't even know if Cash was going to like that vocal group or not, so I made sure to get the records pressed up while he was out of town. I think it kind of surprised him when he heard those *bah-doo-pah-doo*s on there, but he never did say anything about it. And of course everybody else liked it. It was a hit. See, to Sam, I was kind of like Ricky Skaggs is to me, you know what I mean? Slick. I was kind of slick. Sam was more into funk and stuff like that—ragged sounds—and I was somewhere in between.

. . . . *J A N E S* . . . .

Sam had a knack for taking people that probably nobody else in the world would've recorded because they sounded so different and making them stars. Jerry Lee had been to Nashville trying to get a contract and they told him that he should get rid of that piano and get him a guitar. That tells you something. Like Johnny Cash. I don't think anybody would've recorded Johnny Cash.

Johnny Cash was somewhere between country and rockabilly. I don't know what you would classify Johnny as except a hit artist. If you want to get technical, he probably was the most distinct artist, the most unique, of all the artists at Sun. He had

EPA-112

Johnny Cash

A rare photo of Johnny Cash *almost* smiling *(Center for Southern Folklore Archives)*

this guy, Luther Perkins, and he was the most unique guitar player in the world. What he played was so simple, yet no one in the world could play it like Luther. I couldn't play it like Luther. Nobody could. He had his own sound and there wasn't no way you could do it. Johnny and Sam came up with the idea of putting some paper in between the strings on his guitar—under a string, over the next one—and it came up with kind of a snare drum sound. I've said many times that Sam was the only guy in the world to have the nerve enough to go in and cut hit records with a three-piece band.

0

Although Jack Clement's work with Johnny Cash would give the label some of its biggest hits, they would be some of the last he cut at Sun. Following what were perceived by an inebriated Sam Phillips as undermining insults, Clement and his co-producing/arranging buddy Bill Justis ("Raunchy") were given walking papers—or rather, walking letters.

. . . . *CLEMENT*. . . . .

Sam fired me. He fired me and Bill Justis at the same time. It was because he was drunk. He was having a party and we'd been recording all day, working with Bill Justis. And then Sam came in there and was just disrupting everything and sitting out in the studio, crawling in the bass drum case and clowning around. Just really disrupting everything. He really just wanted to hang out. But it was kind of in the early evening, and Bill had been getting drunk. He used to think that he had to drink on those sessions to play that bad, and he had a tendency to get the boys in the band kind of high.

By the time Sam got there, he had had a few, and Bill had had a few, and they got to talking and arguing and all that kind of stuff. And at that time, I had this guy named Cliff Gleaves that Elvis had kicked out of [Graceland]. Well, he had moved in with me and I lived over in Frayser, across the river. So it was time to go, and it was snowing, so I wanted to get home before the bridge iced up. So I walked over to the control room. I was done for the day and Cliff and Sam were in there talking and telling jokes and stuff, and I said, "Come on, Cliff, we've got to go." Meaning, "Hey, man, it's snowing. Let's go." Sam didn't even know it was snowing. But anyway, something between what I'd said that night and what Bill Justis said had made Sam mad, so he wrote us both letters before he left that night. I still have a copy of the thing. You can tell he'd had a few by some of the language.

It basically said we weren't showing respect, et cetera, et cetera. I saw there was another one there for Bill Justis, so I read mine and I called him and said, "I think you got a letter like this."

But I was ready to leave, anyway. I was planning on getting out of there pretty soon, so it didn't matter. I was just ready to move on. I'd written hit records and produced hit records and I could probably come to Nashville and do the same. Actually, Chet Atkins offered me a job one time. He wanted me to move to New York. I'd come over and done a session one time while I was working at Sun. I wanted to cut a record myself but I did not want to cut it in that funky old studio. So I came to Nashville and RCA and hired Bob Moore and I hired a piano player and we cut "Ten Years" and "Loverboy." It had a lot of echo on it. It was kind of a neat sound, and Chet heard it and thought it was great. He said he'd never cut anything like that around there. He was asking me if I might be interested in working at RCA in New York. I said I might, but I didn't really think I would. But he called me a week or two later and said he had set it up for me to go up and meet with Steve Sholes in New York, so I went up. But I didn't really think I wanted to do that. I didn't want to move to New York. But I could've gone up there and been the A&R guy but I didn't want to do it.

Sam and I didn't have any problems. It's just that I was ready to leave there at any time at that point. He'd run all the artists off, and Jerry Lee wasn't selling and there wasn't much happening there. I could've probably gone off and got with Johnny Cash somewhere, moved to wherever he was at and written a bunch of hit songs and worked with him or something. There were places I could've gone because of what I had done at that time. I think Sam kind of sensed that I was ready to go, and he probably sensed that there wasn't nothing happening there either.

But actually the next day Sam offered to set me up in a record deal. I mean, he fired us, but it was kind of like if I had wanted to go back there and say, "Well, let's work this out," it wouldn't have been any problem. But I was ready to go. I never quit going there, though, and I've always stayed in touch with Sam. I always felt like I should do that. Sam's got a perspective on things that nobody else has and I like to have that input into my life. You know what I mean?

. . . . *JIM DICKINSON* . . . . . .

Bill Justis would always laugh and say he was fired for insubordination. But Justis had such a weird personality and such a backward way of looking at things. I do know this: I knew Bill well enough to say that he was pissed. I've never been able to get through with Clement, so I don't know what happened with him and Sam. He and I just push against each other like the white dog and the black dog with the magnets on their feet. We've been around each other a few times, and it doesn't work. I don't know why. I scare some people. I don't think Jack's afraid of me, but at the same time I think he picks up something. I feel a weird vibe from him, I'll be frank with you. He's an interesting man, for sure. And to take nothing away from him, he's a *real* producer. But there's just something that doesn't work between me and him. And with Justis it was totally the opposite. I would've never gotten a break but for Bill Justis, and of course I didn't get it in Memphis, as it was. I got it in Nashville, which was even weirder.

About two years before Clement and Justis were bounced, Billy Lee Riley left the label in an even more acrimonious but typically alcohol-fueled fashion.

. . . . *RILEY* . . . .

Sam and I had a big fight. I was in Canada doing some shows and I had booked myself with Alan Freed, who was going to start a tour in May that year. I called Sam and told him about it, and I had "Red Hot" out and Jerry Lee had "Great Balls of Fire." He said, "Man, close out those shows and come home and let's cut an album to get ready for this tour." I closed out there early and we came all the way home, finally got into the studio here and started doing some things. I was just thrilled to death, you know? I'm going out on the Alan Freed show and they're going to make me a star! I'm gonna be bigger than Elvis!

But I didn't know what was going on behind the scenes. Sam had gotten with Alan Freed and had me kicked off the tour and got Jerry Lee put on the tour instead, because they were pushing him and not me. That was enough to make me mad. I didn't know about that at the time, until after I came in the studio one morning and sat down at the front, and there were three telegram orders from distributors in Detroit and Cincinnati. They had each ordered ten thousnad copies of "Red Hot." Thirty thousand records! Alan Freed had declared it a hit and he was playing it like crazy on WINS and the Hound Dog was playing it in Buffalo, and man, that record was happening like crazy.

So there was "Great Balls of Fire," which Sam was trying to push, and my record, which was already on its way. So when I saw those orders I thought, "Man, I know I'm going to be somebody now. I'm going to tour with Alan Freed. I've got a hit record. There ain't no way I can miss. There's *no way* to miss."

So Sam finally comes into the studio around 1:30 or so in the afternoon, and I'm just thrilled to death, thinking that when he sees those orders he's going to come over and hug me and say, "Man, I got my Elvis here." But what he did instead was, he looked at those orders and called each of the distributors and said, "We're not shipping this number. We're shipping Jerry Lee's 'Great Balls of Fire.' We're putting all our efforts on that, so we're not shipping Billy Riley's record."

I'm standing there listening to that. I'm standing right there in front of him. And when he got through I just looked at him and walked out. I couldn't talk to him. I was hurt. I felt worse, I believe, than I ever felt in my life. And I went out, got in my '57 Chevrolet, and went to West Memphis and bought a Texas fifth of Four Roses. And I started drinking, and I drank and I drank, and I started thinking about some ways to get rid of Sam. Blow his place up, blow *him* up. I pulled over by the river and I sat on the banks and drank my liquor, thinking, "How could somebody do this?" you know? Why would somebody just deliberately throw something away that was a sure thing to go with something that hadn't even started happening. He thought Jerry Lee was the next big phenomenon—the next big Elvis—and he didn't have time for this other stuff, because "Great Balls of Fire" was as different as Elvis was when he came out. I guess he was thinking, "Billy Riley's great, but he's not much different than what everybody else is doing." But I had a *hit record.* That should've made me different.

I finally got back in my car and back on the road and I drove and I drove, all the way to Truman, Arkansas, and I hung around over there till about dark, and I came back and I walked into Sun and I was *drunk.* Sam wasn't there, but Sally, the secretary, was there, and I barged in drunk. I had my courage then. I said, "Where's Sam at?" She said he wasn't there, and I said, "Get him on the phone. I've got to see him." Boy, I was mad. She said, "Billy, I don't know where he is. I can't get him on the phone." So I said, "Well, you better get him on the phone. I want to talk to him." So I went into the back of the studio and wandered around and drank awhile.

J.M. had drove up to the studio, so I started telling him about it and that I wanted to report Sam to the Musicians Union. *Then* Sally called Sam and told him he'd better get down there. I came back into the studio and got on the phone with the president of the union. I said, "I want to tell you some things about Sam Phillips. We've been down there cutting sessions that aren't union." He said, "Billy, why don't you call me on Monday?" and I said, "No, I'm calling you *now*. I want to set up a special session. Sam owes us a lot of money. He's only paying us two dollars an hour for all these sessions and all these hits." So Sally gets on the phone again and says, "Sam, you better get down here. Riley's on the warpath." He said, "Well, lock him in the studio and don't let him out."

In the meantime I went over to the piano and I poured that whiskey right down on those keys, all down that console. I said something like, "You're the piano that Jerry Lee Lewis plays. I think you need a drink." I went into the engineer room and poured whiskey in his Ampex tape recorders, poured it on his board. He had all these file cabinets full of master tapes, so I started shaking that and those tapes were falling on the floor and getting all mixed up. There was a big green chair in the studio, and by then I'm getting pretty drunk, and I sat down in that green chair, almost passing out. Sam finally came in and took me into his office, and he sat in there with his fifth of Vat 69 and I still have what's left of my Four Roses, and he said, "Let's talk this over."

We talked all night until sunup, and Sam convinced me, convinced me totally with his charm. He said, "We've got bigger things planned for you. What we want to do is get this Jerry Lee thing out, get it off our back, get it going, so we can concentrate on *you*. We're going to get you this and that and we're going to make you a big star." By the time I left there the next morning, I was totally convinced that I was his favorite kid and he was protecting me and I was going to be the next star. Then, when I sobered up and realized how things really were, I left Sun and cut one record for Brunswick in 1958 with Owen Bradley, "Rockin' on the Moon." It didn't do anything, though, so I came back to Sun like nothing happened and went out and started cutting records again on the same contract.

See, this was *home*, man. Once you started something here this was home, and I think that was a big fault of mine to think like that. But I felt so good being here and working with who I was working with that to get out of here, I felt like I was an alien. I didn't feel good in Owen Bradley's studio with Owen Bradley behind the controls. I felt good right here and I came back here and did "One More Time," "Got Your Water Boiling," stuff like that, and I stayed at Sun until I left again in late '59.

Upon leaving Sun for good, Riley and Janes hooked up to form the short-lived Rita label, netting a huge pop hit in 1959 with "Mountain of Love," recorded by one-time Sun artist Harold Dorman.

. . . . *J A N E S* . . . .
Sam was in the process of building the new studio at the time and Riley and I went to Sam with the proposition to let us keep the old studio and try to do some records and let him have the product. He was considering it. He probably had so many other things on his mind that he never really got back with us, so we took that as a no. I don't know if it would've been a no or a yes. We never got that far into it. But we decided to start a label on our own, so we rounded up a third party that had a little money, Ira Lynn Vaughan. We didn't have any to speak of. The three of us formed a record label. The way it got its name, this third party had a daughter named Rita, and we were trying to come up with a name, and her picture was sitting on his desk. I said, "What's your daughter's name?" and he said, "Rita," and I said, "That'd be a good name."

Harold Dorman was trying to get a deal with different people and we always thought he was a great songwriter and a good, soulful country singer. So when we started the label, he was one of the first people we decided to record. And we had a pretty good record on him. "Mountain of Love." We recorded it and we released it without all the background on it. I think we just had a rhythm section and Harold, which was okay back then. But in order to try to break it into the bigger markets, they thought we ought to dress it up a bit. So we brought it back into the studio and just overdubbed strings and maybe voices to it. It's the same version, it's just got stuff added to it. You had the basics there already. If you notice, the strings are playing the same thing that the horns are playing. We had Marty Willis on there, one of the greatest musicians who ever came out of Memphis who gets mentioned very little. A great musician. I would not do a session without him there because he was a great idea man. If you got stumped on something, he could come up with ideas and things. He was just a great musician. He worked on "Mountain of Love," several hits with the Bill Black Combo, a bunch of things.

We had some bad luck with Rita. We had been working with a distributor out of Atlanta and we had some financial problems with them and what-have-you. It just kind of broke up. In the meantime we had rented a building with the intention of putting in our own studio, and we got the building rented and the obligation for the building and about a third of the equipment we needed and kind of went broke. That was Sonic. But I was finally able to maneuver around and get it opened and I was in that studio for a number of years and finally got burned out and dropped out of the business for about five years and taught recording.

I taught at Kansas Vocational School. It's a high school; they teach kids from ninth to twelfth grade from different feeder schools, mixed in with adults, so you taught a lot of different people. A friend of mine in town heard that they were looking for an instructor and I wasn't doing that well financially at the time, so I went over there and talked to them and they hired me.

It was interesting, but five years was about all the interest I could handle. The problem I had with teaching was, you could start at a certain level and you worked up to a certain level and then you had to start all over again. It wasn't going anywhere. And too, when you're dealing with the school board, you don't just go out and get the latest equipment, you have to go through all the political stuff and it was just a bit much for me. After five years of that I came back to work at Phillips.

While Janes found his niche at Phillips's new studio, Riley's post-Sun career has been mostly desultory, with a few highlights scattered among a slew of recordings for dozens of labels, with nary a chart hit in the bunch. Riley formed another ill-fated label after the dissolution of Rita, then did radio and jingle work before heading to the West Coast, where he found work as a session musician. (That's him playing lead guitar on Herb Alpert's sixties smash, "The Lonely Bull.") When Sun was reactivated as Sun International following its late-sixties purchase by Shelby Singleton, Riley climbed aboard once again for a few decent sides (most notably "Kay," from 1969) and by 1971 he almost landed a hit for Chips Moman with "I've Got a Thing About You Baby," an excellent white-soul thumper that got lost amid a distribution squabble between Moman and Columbia. (Elvis cut a version of it two years later during the Stax sessions for his *Good Times* album.) Riley resurfaced in 1992 on the independent blues label Hightone with *Blue Collar Blues,* a fine set of redux rockabilly recorded at Sam Phillips's with some of his former bandmates, including Roland Janes and J. M. Van Eaton.

Following Jack Clement's termination from Sun, he hung around Memphis long enough to form an unsuccessful label (Summer Records) before moving to Beaumont, Texas, where he and Bill Hall set up a label and publishing company, raking in some dough via Sun vet Dickey Lee's "Patches" and "She Thinks I Still Care." After making the move to Nashville in 1965, Clement hit his stride as a producer, cutting prime stuff on Waylon Jennings (most notably the groundbreaking 1975 album *Dreaming My Dreams*), Charley Pride, and Don Williams, among many others.

As for Bill Justis, he tried his hand at running a record label following his termination from Sun, but his Play Me Records—despite the persuasive title—was a bomb. After working PR for a trucking line in Memphis, Justis moved to Nashville to do freelance session and A&R work. By 1961 he was producing and arranging for Mercury, and within two years he would cross paths with a young pianist named Jim Dickinson.

FOUR

Dixie Flyer

In a city full of oddball visionaries and brilliant weirdos, Jim Dickinson can right-
fully call Memphis home. Although he's lived for a pretty good while about thirty-
five miles outside of Memphis, in a small Mississippi community between
Coldwater and Hernando, Dickinson has come to embody the reckless spirit and
wild-eyed sense of purpose that define so much music produced in the humid
river town. The pianist and producer has been a crucial, if sometimes overlooked, figure in the city's rock, soul, and blues history since he first started
doing studio work in the early 1960s—from the sad final days of Sun to the
surge of Southern soul and its pop and rock spin-offs via studios such as Stax
and American.

A former member of the crack backing outfit the Dixie Flyers, and a session
man who put his stamp on the Rolling Stones' "Wild Horses" and the seminal
early albums of Ry Cooder, Dickinson's first major studio gig came in 1963 via
a folk album produced by Sun arranger/saxophonist Bill Justis. At the time,
Justis was also at the production board for the two singles recorded at Sun by
Dickinson's Beale Street Shieks (1964's "You'll Do It All the Time") and

Katmandu Quartet ("Monkey Man," from 1965), both of which were issued on Monument's Southtown subsidiary. Dickinson earned hipster points early on for both *Dixie Fried* (his debut album from 1972) and his production of Big Star's *Sister Lovers*. That shambolic downer classic, in many ways a collaborative effort between Dickinson and Big Star auteur Alex Chilton, was recorded in 1974 but belatedly released in 1978; it has now been embraced by the mopey alt-rock brigade as their own *Sgt. Pepper's*. Since then Dickinson has produced fine albums by the Replacements, True Believers, Jason and the Scorchers, and Toots Hibbert; worked with locals ranging from Chilton to boho rockabilly Tav Falco; and intermittently cranked out slopbucket raunch with the ragtag Mud Boy and the Neutrons. He also performs around Memphis with DDT, the band formed by his sons Luther and Cody Dickinson.

A pure product of Memphis dementia, an inheritor of Sam Phillips's legacy and Dewey Phillips's colorblind vision, Jim Dickinson has helped shape the city's past while ambling recklessly into its future. There was a gala event in Memphis held in 1991 in celebration of Dickinson's fiftieth birthday. In the accompanying program, Sam contributed a sonnet:

> Shades of anticipation is the ever-present glint in Jim D.'s eyes. Hearing strange noises that others let pass by.
> Music that makes you shout, walk the backs of gospel benches, makes you moan, yes even cry. It could be, it may be, it is Jim D.'s soul of sound bouncing off the sky, onward and upward, upwards.

"The strange thing about it is, people read this thing and they don't know what he's talking about," Dickinson says some six years after the affair. "But I'll be damned if I don't." After all, you know what they say about like minds.

. . . . *JIM DICKINSON* . . . .

I was born in Little Rock in 1941. Actually conceived in Memphis but born in Little Rock. My family was from Little Rock, so my mother wanted me born there, but I never lived there. We moved to Hollywood, and then Chicago before we came to Memphis when I was almost nine. My father worked for Diamond Match in Chicago. He was a vice president there, and in Memphis he was a district manager and he kind of worked his way down to stay in Memphis. They wanted him to move to New York, but he wanted to bring his family back home. We moved here in 1949, which was just about when things were starting to shift in Memphis.

I'm at least fifth- or sixth-generation musician, although they weren't professionals. They were all trained. My mother was concert-trained. She played piano in church pretty much her whole life. They started out trying to teach me piano when I was about four and a half, maybe five years old, but I have real bad eyes, and had no glasses at the time. I had this really hot-shot teacher in Chicago. I remember his white hair and his little narrow fingers, but I don't remember his name. He kept talking to me about dots and spots, but I wasn't seeing any spots. All I was seeing was a smear. So I started to play by ear. My mother had been a teacher, so she tried to teach me as well, but it was real frustrating for her. None of it made any sense to me until we came to the South and I encountered black music and found a pattern that I could learn to play.

I had two really major experiences before that. One was seeing what turned out to be the Memphis Jug Band—Will Shade and Charlie Burse. Of course, I didn't know that's who it was then. They were playing in the alley behind where my father's office was, which was Park Lane, and Whiskey Chute ran between it—they called it Whiskey Chute from the Prohibition days. It ran from Main Street to Front Street. It was the area where I played as a child—uptown. On Saturday afternoons I would go uptown with my father, and there was a magic store back in there and a hobby shop and an old barber shop, and one day I saw the Jug Band sitting there playing "Come On Down to My House," and it was the damndest thing I'd ever seen. I was already into music, but this was the strangest music I'd ever heard, and from that point on I wasn't very interested in many things except finding that music. Which of course was just down the street, but in 1950, 1951, it was inaccessible to a little white kid.

The other experience I had was seeing Howlin' Wolf in a warehouse in West Memphis, Arkansas. I didn't know for years that it was Howlin' Wolf, but that's who it was. I figured it out just through deductive reasoning. The warehouse was where the KWEM radio station used to be. My father was in a warehouse counting clothes pins with some client and I heard the music. I followed it to an open door and there were these four black guys playing this weird music at the radio station.

Before I came to Memphis, radio was radically segregated. But there was a guy on the radio in Chicago named Two-Ton Baker the Music Maker, who was a piano player. Other than my mother, he was my original influence. He would play the piano while he did the news or the weather or whatever. While he was interviewing someone he'd play the piano. It gave me a musical-dialogue idea that I've kind of kept running throughout various parts of my career. It just appeals to me—the idea of talking with musical accompaniment, you know?

But when we came to Memphis, like everybody my age, or every white kid my age, I learned about the blues—WDIA and the black radio stations—through our yardman. I was probably eleven or twelve at the time. Alec the yardman, he had taught me everything he could teach me. He was a great singer but he couldn't play an instrument, so he brought me these men who could. Having already taught me how to shoot dice and throw a knife and all the things that a smart-aleck, Yankee-talking kid should learn, which was really what he was doing. He was acclimatizing me to my new environment.

He's the one who first brought around the piano player who actually taught me to play. There were two of them, actually. One guy named Butterfly and the other guy I only know as "Dishrag." As Dishrag he was semi-famous. People around Memphis will talk about Dishrag. Butterfly's actual name was something Washington—I don't know what his first name actually was. They all had nicknames back then. Butterfly was the most colorful of the two, but Dishrag actually showed me the thing that I learned to play with, which was he said that everything in music is made up by the "codes." And I thought he meant like secret codes, like Captain Midnight, which I was young enough to be into. And I thought, "Well hell, no wonder I couldn't do this. It's a damn code! Nobody ever told me it was a code." Of course, he meant "chords." He said, "This is how's you makes a code. You take any note, and you go three up and four down, just like in poker." And he didn't mean musical steps; he meant keys on the piano. If you go three up and four down on any note on the piano, it makes a major triad and your thumb always lands on the key signature note. When I saw that I thought, "Well, by God, I can do that. *That* makes sense. All this E–G–B–D–F crap doesn't make much sense to me, but *this* makes sense." And of course if you take a chord with your right hand and an octave with your left hand—and I already knew what an octave was—and play it back and forth in a syncopated rhythm, you have rock and roll. All you have to do is start to run the chord with your left hand and, by God, it's boogie-woogie. And depending on how you handle the eighth-notes, it can be a shuffle. It was right there for me. That's how I learned to play the piano. And I still play in major triads. It's the way I think, and it makes it real easy to play with a guitar player.

I started playing along to the radio and playing to records like everyone else, because there was no way you could go to a music store and learn to play rock and roll in 1952, 1953. Hell, there *wasn't* any rock and roll to play. Music to my mother was a gift from God, which it is, and she was dead set against me becoming a musician—which is probably why I became one.

The idea of being a professional musician didn't cross my mind until well into college, although I had a band before then. I formed my first band, The Regents, in 1958 to play on a talent show at White Station High School. Rock and roll was still very, very young. At the talent show there were two bands, and I had the best guitar players by far, and the other band had the best drummer and two singers. Well, I ended up with the drummer and the two singers when the talent show was over. They had a female piano player, which in 1958 was not cool. Now it would be very hip, but back then I had that band shut down. The singers were like ducktail pretty boys. My first band was instrumental. We played Duane Eddy, Link Wray—instrumental music—and we barely had enough to play a set.

So we got these two pretty-boy ducktail singers, one of whom was Charles Hines, who's now the minister of music at Central Church, and the other is Ronnie Stoots, who became Ronnie Angel and toured with the Mar-Keys years later. We started playing high school dances. There were only two or three nonprofessional bands in the city and they were all basically North Memphis hoodlums. The East Memphis mamas would not let their little virginal daughters hire these greasy North Memphis thugs to play their parties, so my band got the jobs. My wife had a half-brother named Al Stamps, who was one of my inspirations. He was a keyboard player in an East Memphis band that predated mine, but they, like all the other bands in town, played something besides rock and roll. They would play Dixieland, what we would call country club music. Legitimate songs. We couldn't play any of that. All we could play was rock and roll, and I had a set of blues that we would play late at night when I wanted the audience to leave. When the audience stopped leaving when I played the blues, I knew something was happening, that something was changing. That was in about 1960, when people would actually come up and request Jimmy Reed songs rather than shriek in horror.

See, what people lose sight of in the contemporary world is that in 1959 it was not all right for white kids in East Memphis to play black music. With Elvis, it didn't matter. That was something professional and we were doing something that was not. There was no place for teenage music yet. It took the Beatles and the Rolling Stones to legitimatize what we did. There were certainly no groupies. It was not even cool. What we did was deviant behavior of some kind.

Our sets were Sun rockabilly and what I thought then was Chicago blues—Muddy Waters, Howlin' Wolf, Chuck Berry, and the like. I heard it all through Dewey Phillips. I knew Howlin' Wolf had come from West Memphis, but I didn't know that a lot of that stuff had been recorded in Memphis and released in Chicago, and that all of the music was basically Delta music, because it was referred to as Chicago music then. But I was aware of Sun right away because of Dewey. Dewey is where it all came from. My whole musical taste, what I do for a living, came from listening to Dewey Phillips on the radio, because the idea behind what he was doing was so radically different. He was playing white music and black music back to back and was playing it for an integrated audience. And in 1958, 1959, there was no such thing as an integrated audience. And it wasn't even conceptual to him. He was basically such a simple person. He used to yell out on the radio all these idiotic phrases—it was just part of what he did—and one of the things he would say was, "Oh, good people," because that's what he was talking to, see? He was talking to good people—not white people, not black people. Dewey Phillips, in his drug-addicted mind, he was speaking to a one-colored audience, and that color was good, and he was playing good music. It was Sister Rosetta Tharpe and then Hank Williams and then "Tell Me Why You Like Roosevelt"— shit you never heard anywhere else on Earth but Dewey Phillips's radio show.

Another thing Dewey would say was, "It's a hit!" and then play the record, and no one else in the world was hearing that record but people within two hundred miles of Memphis. And I thought they were hits. I thought Billy Riley's "Red Hot" was a hit record until I went to Texas and found out that nobody there had heard it. I could sing it with a band in Texas and people would think it was real good. All of a sudden I had all this arcane information that I thought everybody on earth had. Sonny Burgess? I thought he was a star. Dewey said he was, you know?

Radio had a whole different feeling back then than it has now. People talked music and the radio stations played fifty, sixty, or a hundred records. Nowadays they play ten. They used to talk to the artist, talk about the artist, and have fun. The deejays had fun back then. Now you listen to the radio and you might as well be listening to a cassette recording. A lot of the programming that you hear is the same. It's programmed off a satellite and you've got maybe a dozen consultants who control the whole music industry. It's kind of like back on Dick Clark's show, you had your whole career on the line and a bunch of kids are judging your record. "I give it a fifty and you're out of the business." There's something a little bit unfair about that.

You had several distinct personalities. Dewey Phillips was just one of them. Each field of music had its star in each town and they were distinct. When you heard one you knew exactly who you were listening to. Nowadays, doggone—I was talking to someone today about it. I kid about it, but I think that each major record label has got four basic music tracks: a boy fast track and a boy slow track, and a girl fast track and a girl slow track and they just run the singers and dub them onto the same track. That's what it sounds like. That's not true but it sounds that way sometimes. They use the same licks and the same musicians and everything. There's nothing wrong with that if you try to come up with a sound, but they're in such a situation. They have to do it good and do it quick and get it over with and run into the next one. They cut great-sounding records, but they're not that unique.

I left Memphis in 1960. I graduated from high school in 1960 and went to Baylor in Waco, Texas, the armpit of the universe. It was a real shock for me to leave Memphis and realize how unhip most of the rest of the world was by comparison. Memphis celebrates the individual. It's real easy to see. It's not just in the music. All the success that's come from Memphis has been individual success, and that's why I stay.

I was in Waco two and a half miserable years. I came back in 1963 and went to Memphis State because it was all-important that you stay in school so you didn't go to Vietnam. But when I went to school in Texas, I figured that music for me was over. My best guitar player had been drafted in '59, and the band had pretty much broken up by my senior year of high school, primarily because of teenage alcoholism. We were still playing a lot but it had gotten to be less serious than it had been. I figured it was over when I went to Texas. But I had never had a regular bass player in Memphis, and the first guy I met in Texas was a bass player! I was there in drama school. It seems like an unreasonable place for me to go—Baylor University, the biggest Baptist school on earth—but at the time they had a world-famous drama school and I was really interested in set design. After the first week, all the freshmen in the drama department had to go through freshman tryouts, and they asked at the bottom of the tryout card to list all the musical instruments that you played. So I listed them and before the week was out I was playing drums in the pit band for *Where's Charley?*

I got into studio work completely by accident. When I came back from Baylor I wasn't quite through with theater. The summer of '63, me and two other guys ran a real small student-ish theater at the corner of Cleveland and Poplar, and we put on one-act plays. Each night there would be a one-act play and a folk singer. In '63 folk music was just starting to really boom, but before the summer was over it had taken over and we were just barely doing the plays. At the end of that summer, in order to pay our bills, we had what we called the First Annual Memphis Folk Festival at the Municipal Shell. We had this thing with literally just one ad in the newspaper and one TV promotion and it was full. It caused a traffic jam. They had cops out there at six o'clock turning people away, and nobody on the show was anybody anyone had ever heard of. It was just the people who had worked for me all summer in the theater—Sid Selvidge, Horace Hall, Bob Frank, people who later had careers. But because of the traffic jam, we got

some local publicity. Bill Justis, who was in Nashville by then, picked up on it because of this publicity, and I was asked to come up to Nashville to do this folk record. It was Bill Justis and orchestra and chorus, the Jordanaires, Boots Randolph, and Bill Purcell—all the real Nashville cats were at the session. I had no business being there, but I was the "folk" part of it. It was my first professional session, and it turned into a record contract with Justis and my first record, which was the Beale Street Shieks' "You'll Do It All the Time."

I had been aware of Justis before then. Actually I was more aware of Justis as a musician than of any of the other Sun people for sure, because he was from East Memphis, from a Germantown family. And of course his band. He had what you would call now a society orchestra. They were a little more accessible to me where I lived and more a part of my everyday experience. I remember seeing him at the Colonial Country Club twice with his big band. I remember seeing Mose Allison playing trumpet with him then, before Mose was anybody. I was aware of individuals in his band—Cowboy Drain, the trombone and bass player, and Sid Lapworth. I don't know what it was except that they were more professional and in a way just more accessible than these redneck guys who were the rest of the Sun artists.

Justis, of course, has a reputation for hating rock and roll, which I don't really think is true. He had a real attitude about it, but he had a real attitude about everything. I don't think Justis hated rock and roll. He resented it, for sure, and the records he made were made with contempt. But I think a lot of people did that, and I think that the aspect of jazz musicians playing down to rock and roll is one of the things that's missing from it now. Talk to Jerry Wexler about the way they made the early R&B records and he'll tell you that they would hire a blues band and one jazz player and let the jazz guy take the solo.

Justis was just kind of sarcastic. He was a joker, always joking and bullshitting. I think he introduced bop talk into the rock and roll jargon. Two great credits that I can give to Justis, although they're both pretty obscure, is that, and effing. Effing is a thing that, as popular as it ever got in Nashville was because of Justis, and I think Justis learned it from Harmonica Frank Floyd and took it to Nashville. Effing is like making rhythmic noises with your mouth, and as far as I'm concerned, Harmonica Frank Floyd at least introduced it to our area. Justis must have picked it up from him.

And just by picking that up, it shows that while he belittled in a way what Sam Phillips was doing, he must have been fascinated by it at the same time, because so much of it was reflected in his career. I think Sam realized he needed somebody who was a professional musician, who could read and write and who could handle a little more than he could handle. Justis was the kind of person that, it was a door that opened, so he went through it.

Of course, "Raunchy" was the first hit. You'll hear a lot of different versions of this, but the melody of "Raunchy," such as it is, was actually written by an organ player from Berclair, out in East Memphis, named Littlefield. He ran a jewelry store and was a piano tuner. He was basically ripped off for the idea of the "Raunchy" melody. The guitar lick. And it's not all Sid

Manker, it's Sid Manker *and* Roland. It's two guitars. Simple as it is, you can't do it on one guitar. It's like, here's the jazz guy going *daw-daw,* there's the redneck going *dang,* and that was Justis's whole idea of music. Roland still really resents a lot of the Justis stuff, because he takes a lot of Justis's jokes real personally still. Just his attitude, the anti-rock and roll attitude. Justis was the first person I've ever heard call a whole room full of musicians "girls." He'd say, "Okay, girls, let's cut a session."

That was just his personality. It was just the way he talked about music. I think he had a little contempt for rock and roll but it was just part of his personality. I think he would've been

that way about any kind of music. It wasn't like a disdainful contempt. He was the hipster jazz guy for sure, but it wasn't the same kind of looking down on the music. I don't know how to describe the difference, but Justis was no great jazz musician. He was a mediocre big-band guy, you know? He had no great artistic viewpoint to look down on rock and roll from. He was an entertainer pure and simple. A little more than a journeyman because he was a leader, a definite *band* leader and could lead a roomful of musicians who were all better than he was.

Justis didn't actually call me for that first session. A trumpet player that I had known from high school, George Tidwell, was the one who called me. I don't know whether Justis saw the thing in the paper about the festival himself or whether somebody showed it to him, but he knew about it and he had Tidwell call me. Tidwell had helped me several times in the past—in school and as a musician both. He was in my brother-in-law's band and was a little older than me. And Tidwell always thought I was funny, and Justis did too, basically, as did Bill Black. They just thought I was crazy and funny. And Justis, he took me into the session without even hearing my voice. It was strictly on the basis of my personality and in the publicity in the paper. That was all he knew about me because he had never heard me sing into a microphone. But like I said, it was a big session. Literally all the cats on it—the old-school cats. Five or six guitars. It was a true Nashville session; everybody was reading charts, which my friend Tidwell was writing.

Justis was delighted with me, but I did the wrong thing. When he talked to me beforehand, he semi-described this concept he had. The name of the album was *Dixieland Folk-Style*, a party record, and there was a hit at the time called "Midnight in Moscow," which was like a Dixieland instrumental. And he said it was going to be kind of like that. He said, "Get you two more folk singers and come on along to Nashville." Well, I made the mistake of getting two *good* singers, but he wanted two more like me. I got this man-and-wife team called Colin and Kay, who were kind of loungey folk singers, you know, but both real good. And Justis already had the four Jordanaires and three women from the Anita Kerr Singers, and he had all the *good* voices he wanted. So I ended up doing the whole album and stayed on and overdubbed my voice on several other things. The first time I'd ever overdubbed.

I have to predicate this with the fact that Justis definitely was not a racist, but his term for what I did, which stuck with me the rest of my career with Justis, was "niggabilly." He'd hit the talk-back and say, "Dickinson, give me some more of that niggabilly." And it really is sort of what I do. I mean, he was smart enough to nail me. But it was a great experience for me because it was my first real professional session and it was at a real high level. It was in the Columbia B studio in Nashville.

When I got back to Memphis after the session—and at this point I was a pretty folky, purist type—I said, "Well, this is cool, but my name's not going to be on it, is it?" And he said, "No, no credits." So I said, "Okay. Good." So I went back home and I got this contract in the mail. I called Justis and said, "What's this for?" He says, "Well, don't you want to make a record?" I said, "Well, didn't we just do that?" He said, "No, *you*. Don't *you* want to make a record?" And I said sure, and he said, "Sign the contract and send it back." So I did and we set up a date to record at Phillips. He said, "I'm going to send you one song. You do this song and then you can do anything else you want to do." So he sent me a tape of this song and a mimeographed sheet of lyrics and I hated it. It was just awful, exactly the type of thing I could not do. It was a Shel Silverstein song that was subsequently a big hit record called "The Unicorn" by some Irish group. It's the legend of why there's no more unicorns. It's just so inane. I thought, "What am I going to do with this song?" because I really didn't like it, so I just acted like I didn't get it. But I knew that if I wasn't going to do what Justis wanted me to do, I was going to have to come up with something pretty fucking good.

I thought of the jug band, which had been my original musical inspiration as a child seeing Will Shade. I had just been to Cambridge and had seen Jim Kweskin and the Holy Modal Rounders, and I thought, "Well, if those white Yankees can do it, I can do it, too." So I thought about who I knew that could play a washboard, and Jimmy Crossthwait had been a drummer. He played in the Counts and a couple other bands, but he never played in the traditional way. He would come into your house and play the furniture at that point. He didn't really have an instrument. I saw him play a ceiling fan in rhythm once, and I thought, "By God, I bet Jimmy Crossthwait could play the crap out of a washboard," so I got him and went to a hardware store and got a washboard. And we had another friend from high school who was a guitarist named George Gillis, and it was the same thing—I just made up a zinc-tub bass and gave it to him and said, "Look, just beat this thing like a drum." This was a Thursday afternoon. We played a gig on Friday night at the old Peanut Bar, and Saturday morning we recorded.

When we were recording, Justis didn't come to town for it, and it was supposed to be a demo. So he had time booked down at Phillips's, and it was me, Crossthwait, and Gillis.

Crossthwait had hair over his shoulders even then. This was before the Beatles. And I guess Scotty Moore never did trust me. We had a kind of unfortunate incident about his guitar one night. But Bill Black always liked me, and Scotty and Bill were down there but nobody had really cleared the session. Nobody really believed I was supposed to be there. Scotty thought I was hustling them, so he calls Justis in Nashville and Justis says, "No, this is supposed to be happening." There was no engineer there, so they got Bill Rauzy, who was the tech at the time, and as far as I know that's the only thing he's ever recorded. There were two microphones up but I'm pretty sure the second one wasn't on, so we all got around this RCA Victor microphone and put these four songs down. But then they wouldn't give me the tape. Again, Scotty Moore didn't trust me, so he said, "No, I'll take the tape to Justis myself."

What happened with Scotty was, back in 1959, I guess, when Wink Martindale left Memphis. He had been a disc jockey and TV personality on WHBQ and they had a party out at the Casino, which was a dance hall at the Mid-South Fairgrounds. So at this Wink Martindale farewell party they had Thomas Wayne, he was the big star. Had the song "Tragedy." Scotty and Bill had just quit Elvis within weeks of this so they were out there, and George Klein was the emcee, and Warren Smith was on it, and Anita Wood—Elvis's ex-girlfriend—was there as a personality.

Everyone was playing with the same band, which was Scotty, Bill, and Thomas Wayne's band, except for Kimball Coburn, who was the first of the local clean-cut rock and rollers, so you could call him a puke, I guess. That's sort of what he was. We were his backup band. It always humiliated me, but we had degenerated into that in 1959. Nobody would play with him. He'd get down and do this fruity dance and it was really embarrassing. He had a local hit called "Cute," to give you an idea. It had four chords in it, which at the time was one too many. You should have two songs if you're going to have four chords. But it did get us better gigs, so there we were playing this show with him and Scotty and Bill and everybody.

We were all doing two sets, and our set was one song by me, two songs by Ronnie Stoots, and two songs by Kimball, and of course my song was first. So the first set I did "Send Me Some Lovin'," the Little Richard song, and Warren Smith came up to me afterwards backstage to compliment me—the first time I'd gotten a compliment from someone serious. He said, "You sound like a black guy." I said, "Thank you, Warren." And I did at the time, compared to most white kids. Bill Black wound up playing bass with us, because like I said we never had a permanent bass player. He always liked me. He kind of singled me out. I think he thought I was nuts. But he came up to me backstage and said, "You got a bass player yet?" I said, "No, we still don't have one," and he said, "I just got a new electric bass." Hell, I'd never even *seen* an electric bass. But he asked if I wanted him to play with us, and I said, "Sure, man," so he played with us the first set.

We're playing along and we get to Kimball's first song, "Cute," and I was playing an upright piano with no pickup, just a microphone stuck in the strings. Well, Bill leans over and he says to me, and right into the microphone, says, "What's the name of this song?" and it goes out over the P.A., and I said, "Cute," and he looks down at me and says, "Never heard it," and just goes right on playing it.

So we get to the second set, and we managed to get reasonably drunk between sets. Everybody had. Here we are playing with Bill Black, so we decided we were going to rock and roll. Our big showstopper at the time, the last song we'd play, would be a twenty-five-minute version of "Bo Diddley," and we were the only people in town who knew how to play it in open tuning right. So Ricky Ireland, the guitar player, says, "Let's reverse this set and you go on last and do 'Bo Diddley.'" I said, "Sure, man, but I don't have my guitar." Ricky gets this evil grin on his face and says, "I'm sure Scotty will lend you his." Well, Scotty had this big beautiful Gibson, a gorgeous guitar, and some kind of special amplifier with a bunch of shit in it. He reluctantly let me play his guitar, so the first thing I do is strap on Scotty Moore's guitar and start to retune it, and there he is offstage saying, "No! No!" From that point on he didn't trust me.

So when we showed up to cut this session, he didn't believe it, and even after he talked to Justis, he thought it was just so squirrelly. There we were, these weird pre-hippies, whatever you'd want to call us, doing this strange jug-band music. Scotty didn't understand it. Bill thought it was great. He kept calling people on the phone and having them come down and look at us—to look at Crossthwait, because he did not look like the average person at that time.

So they won't give me the tape. I forgot about it for a while and finally a week or so went by and I called Justis and said, "Did you get that tape? Scotty was kind of weird about it." And Justis said, "Oh yeah, the tape is great. The record comes out on Thursday." I said, "Justis, that was the *demo*, and he said, "Oh no, man, you could never do it that bad again." I was totally mad. I said, "Bill, you have no concept of how bad I could do it." But the record came out on Thursday of the week when the Beatles were on Ed Sullivan for the first time on that Sunday, and it was all over. I got reviewed in *Cashbox* and *Billboard* and everybody in Nashville thought the record was a hit. Then the American music industry stopped for six months. I've always been known for my timing.

Then we cut the session for "Monkey Man," which Bill produced and Sam engineered. It was the Mar-Keys rhythm section and me, recording on Madison Avenue in like '65. This is Charlie Freeman, Duck Dunn, Terry Johnson, and me and Don Nix and Sid Selvidge singing background. Justis and Sam are in the control room, and Sam was all jet-black with sunglasses on and like three days drunk already. He basically didn't come out of the control room but two or three times, and he never took his sunglasses off. So they listened to us awhile, we're jamming around, and finally Justis hits the talk-back and he says, "You boys want to cut this session wet or dry?" And Charlie Freeman, who has also yet to take off his sunglasses, screams out, "Wet!" So from that point on, they would bring a fifth of Old Crow and sit it on this stool in the middle of the studio, and when it was empty another one would appear. We got so wasted Duck took off all his clothes except his pants, and we ended up to trading instruments. It was a great session. That was my introduction to Sam that night.

Dickinson's third session at Sun was held in early 1966, with the young pianist acting as ad hoc vocalist for the Jesters, which featured Sam's younger son, Jerry Phillips, on rhythm guitar. The session—which produced the A-side of one of the last Sun singles ever issued—also marked the debut engineering effort by Sam's eldest boy, Knox Phillips.

. . . . *DICKINSON*. . . . .

The real Jesters had basically broken up. Teddy Paige, the guitar player from the original band, had re-formed the band around Jerry Phillips with some younger players, and they had a singer named Tommy Minga. They cut a bunch of stuff, but Sam wouldn't put any of it out because he hated Minga's voice. I had known Paige a long time, and I had made one, if not two, of the Justis records at this point. So Paige tells me to come down, that I'm going to play piano on this demo session at Phillips's. It was actually Knox's first job as an engineer. So I show up and we wait around and wait around, and I realized that obviously Minga wasn't going to show up because nobody had called him. Paige pulled out a couple sheets of notebook paper and said, "Well, we're down here, let's do something. Why don't you sing it?" So we did four songs that night with Knox, including "Cadillac Man."

When Sam heard it, he liked it. He got all excited, wanted to run the session through the union. So Sam calls me up later, says, "We're going to run it through the union. We're going to cut a smoker session." I figure we're going to sit around and smoke or talk or whatever. I figure it's like a union thing. Well, we get there and Sam is all jacked up. He's wearing a suit and a tie and I'd never seen him wearing anything but all black and sunglasses up to this point. He was totally sober and all businesslike, walking around with a clipboard writing down where the microphones were pinned up. It wasn't like him at all. Then I realized we were going to record again, so we recorded four more songs, one of which was "My Babe," which was the B-side of "Cadillac Man." The other three we cut with Sam have been lost. There were the four that Knox cut, "Jim Dandy," "Sweet Sixteen," and "Night Train from Chicago," and something else, and "Cadillac Man," and then "My Babe," which Sam cut. But there was a song called "Black Cat Bone" that's missing, and two other songs I can't remember.

When they decided to put the record out, Sam called me up. I was already working over at Ardent, which was then in John Fry's house. I had been working before with Chips Moman at the old American studio. At that time the whole American rhythm section was Tommy Cogbill, me, and Clarence Nelson—and Clarence had to sweep up also! But I went from there to Ardent because Fry had more equipment in that house on Grandview than Chips had in his studio, and I figured that Fry would eventually let me run the board and Chips wouldn't. And after I'd quit Chips, the first person he hired was an engineer, which shows you how good my timing is. And then Fry told me, "Jim, I don't think you're emotionally suited to be an engineer." He was right, but it took me a couple of years to figure that out.

But Sam called and said, "We're going to put this record out, boy. You've got to cast your lot." I said, "Sam, I'm afraid my lot's already cast. I'm under contract with Bill Justis." Sam said, "Hell, man, Bill won't care." Sure enough, Bill didn't care, and they put the record out.

The Jesters' one and only single, "Cadillac Man"/"My Babe," was issued on February 1, 1966. With a blistering vocal by Dickinson and the drunken intensity of a primo Billy Lee Riley session, "Cadillac Man" was anomalous, to say the least, arriving just as young rock and rollers in America were beginning to flirt with psychedelia. Nevertheless, the song picked up a little airplay around Memphis and even found its way to the turntable of Dewey Phillips.

. . . . DICKINSON . . . .

First time I ever heard myself on the radio was when Dewey Phillips played "Cadillac Man" and I almost had a fucking car wreck. I had to pull over. The record did nothing, but Dewey played it. Said, "Here's another payola record," and played it. I heard him play it twice, actually. It was a little better than the first time I was on the radio. I didn't hear it, but somebody told me about it. The first time they played my jug-band record on WLAC in Nashville, it was played by John Richberg, and I'm sure it was out of a favor to Justis. He played it two nights in a row. The first night he said, "There's some kind of disturbance out here in the parking lot. Wait a minute, I'm going to stick a microphone out the window and see what it is," then he played my record. And the next time he said, "I've been in the music business for twenty-five years and this is without a doubt the worst record I've ever heard," and played my record again. It's a fine piece of work, let me tell you.

Sun was virtually over by the time of the Jesters record. This was the last-gasp attempt, really. Sam and Jud had some kind of deal where Jud went out on the road doing promotion, but it was a different world. They just weren't geared up for the reality of 1966. Nor was the music. It was antique music already by then. Hell, that's why they liked it. Sam liked it because it sounded old.

He was just way past it. It had been over, really, since 1960, 1961. When he moved away from 706, I don't think Sam ever felt the same way about it. It was largely Stan Kesler's success, the success from the new studio. It wasn't even really Sam's doing. I've heard the story about the move. It's as simple as them losing the lease. And by '58 Sam had made a sizable amount of money—not a whole lot, but enough to try it on his own. The other place set there empty for years. It was a garage for a while. Jim Blake and I broke into it one night and recorded there, and you could feel it. Of course, now it's a tourist trap, but even then, with the cars parked around and the wall torn down, you could feel it. It's a very special place.

Justis called me not long before he died and asked me if I had a copy of "You'll Do It All the Time." I said, "Bill, I've got one but it's cracked." He said, "No, I mean the tape," and I had no idea where the tapes were. Still don't. He said he had been listening to the stuff from his old publishing company and that he decided—he always thought that record was eleven years ahead of itself. He always said that, and why he said "eleven" I'll never know. He said people had just caught up to it and he wanted to put it out again. He was dead in three months.

FIVE

706 Union Avenue

It is a tourist trap now, the place where Sam Phillips and his odd cast of bluesmen and rockers helped to carve out the bedrock of rock and roll. But what you
notice first when you walk into Sun studio—adorned today with enlarged black-
and-white photos of Elvis, Jerry Lee Lewis, et al—is how small the place is.
Then you notice, as you're standing within its measly dimensions, how nonde-
script it is. Just four walls, a ceiling, a tiny reception area in front that leads to
the actual studio, and finally another room in the back that housed the equipment. Even in the 1950s it couldn't have seemed like much.

Maybe that's one reason the music that was produced in this modest but uni-
versally lauded facility came out the way it did: Free of the intimidation and
excessive self-consciousness that the recording process can bring, the musicians
who recorded at Sun felt enough at ease to do what they did with at least a
measure of comfort; whether it took two, twelve, or twenty takes to find the
right way to nail the right song.

Phillips strived to create that kind of atmosphere at Sun. By most accounts,
the sessions were loose, and he worked closely, patiently, with his artists, push-

ing them to reach whatever potential they had. Phillips's method was in accordance with his belief that to get the best out of the dirt-poor sharecroppers and poorly educated Southerners who came to him, he had to let them know that, as he told writer Peter Guralnick in the late seventies, "I was part of the total effort."

No doubt there. Just as his pioneering recording techniques (ranging from mike placement to his tape-delay slapback echo) added to the nuance and over-all sound of his productions, Phillips's ear more times than not told him when a song was there, or merely halfway there. Examples abound on the numerous collections of complete Sun sessions currently available, but the best may be Carl Perkins's "Blue Suede Shoes." The outtakes from that session, available on the Bear Family boxed set *The Classic Carl Perkins,* chronicle a masterpiece on its way from great to simply perfect. A lesser producer might have opted to release the first or third take—both are fine—but Phillips knew it was the second version that best defined what Perkins wanted to do with the song. And it became a rockabilly benchmark and one of rock and roll's greatest hits.

A lot of writers and critics have celebrated Phillips's supposed ability to work with his artists as equals, but little evidence exists to support that line of thinking (despite his documented admiration for many of the men he produced and recorded). There's no reason to think that the relationship between Phillips and his artists was anything more than that of producer and artist working toward the same goal—to cut hit records. Of course, that didn't happen much at Sun: Amazingly enough, considering the overwhelming quality of the average Sun release, the label produced only thirty-five singles that cracked *Billboard*'s R&B, country, or pop charts, and never landed a number one pop hit. But if hit records were all that mattered, there would be a lot more talk about the relative merits of Three Dog Night, and Sun would be regarded as simply the place where Elvis first started making records.

But something happened in that small room on a regular basis, something that would forever change the way people heard, felt, and responded to popular music—something that never quite happened after Phillips moved Sun to its new, high-tech facility in the early 1960s. Some of the men who recorded at Sun say there's a kind of magic to the old place—a vibe, an electricity in its ambience that remains even today. Others remember it as just a place where you could cut records. They're all right, but one fact still remains: There was something about that room.

There was no engineer at the sessions per se. Sam Phillips *was* the engineer. He was everything. We didn't have any session time booked. We just picked a day that we were going to go in there and we went in there and cut it. You didn't have no special time to get there, in a sense, and no special time to leave, so we'd go in, set up, start playing. Sam would turn the damn tape recorder on, and just record.

I had all the freedom in the world there. Every song that I recorded with Sun, there was nothing arranged or written out. We did it all right there in the studio. And whatever we came up with when we were through was what we had. Sometimes we'd stay in there all night. We would discuss what we were going to name the song, and if you notice, some of the earlier material has some of the same lyrics, because after a while just standing at the microphone trying to think of something as you go, it's kind of hard to come up with fresh lyrics every time.

I have to say that one thing that made it unique at Sun was that it was raw. There was nothing dressed up, no sophisticated machines, you know? No big band arrangements. None of that stuff. We just played what we felt and used what we had to and that's what came out. You might say it was more relaxed then. Today, you have certain times that you need to be in the studio from beginning to end because you're paying for the time. The difference then, though, was you would just go in there and whatever time it took, that was the time you had. We didn't have no producer or anything. Ike Turner was there at the very first couple of sessions to say, "You should maybe do it this way or that way." After that, I was basically on my own. If you wanted to call him a producer, you could call him that, but it'd be better to say he was a little negotiator and something like an A&R person that brought you in and saw to it that you started out doing what you wanted to do. Like an advisor type.

You'd go in the studio and you didn't have to worry about if you're going to get a hit record. When you come into the studio he would say, "Don't try to make a hit record, try to make a good one." That's what I always did. You'd go into the studio at seven, eight o'clock at night and come out at four, five o'clock in the morning, but when you'd come out he'd say, "You've got it."

The Biharis let you do whatever you wanted to do. If you got it, good, if you don't, too bad. Whereas Sam, he was demanding. He wanted you to record to his satisfaction. The Biharis, they just wanted Rosco, that's all—good, bad, indifferent, they just wanted Rosco. I believe that Sam knew what he wanted, and knew what he wanted out of me, so he would keep me there until he got that out of me. I felt like anything I did was good, because at that time everything I did was a hit. I don't mean they were multimillion sellers, nothing like that, but they'd do a half a million, quarter-million. And at that time that was a lot of records and a lot of money.

It's funny. Sam had all that rinky-dink recording stuff, he didn't have but one track, but it's amazing the sound that man could get out of that one track.

I tell you, Jack Clement worked with finesse. He was one of the greatest engineers, and we actually respected him more than we respected Sam. If he'd say, "Let's try this," we'd try that. And if we'd cut something that sounded good, he'd say, "Come in here and listen to this. We got a *hit*." He'd always say we had a hit, whether it was or not. Jack was one of the easiest guys to work with that I've ever worked with. He would even come out there during a session and dance around on the floor while the session was going on, or maybe even pick up a guitar and play something.

In this studio, we never did a session out there unless most of us were completely drunk, bombed out. We didn't do dope, though. We would just drink, and most of the time we walked in there we'd have what we wanted, we'd have our drinks, and by the time the sessions was over everybody was stoned.

Usually, a session would get started about one o'clock in the afternoon. First thing, we'd be next door at Taylor's having lunch or something. I'd bring a bottle of wine or maybe a bottle of whiskey to the studio, and if Sam was around he always had some Vat 69, so we didn't have to worry about that. And there was always plenty of beer. We'd take a break and somebody would go get a six-pack. We'd always have what we'd need.

Ninety-nine percent of the time nobody would know what we were going to do when we walked in. Nobody had a plan, nobody would say, "Here's the songs, here's the chord progressions, here's all we need, let's do it this way." Jack would just set up the mikes out there and we'd start playing. Somebody'd say, "Anybody know what song we can do?" or somebody would say, "Well, I heard this song," or, "What do you think about this?" And maybe once in a blue moon Sam would say, "Here's an old record of a blues I want you to listen to." Until Jerry Lee started getting pretty big and there were songs coming from outside writers, we didn't have anything to work on. We were just jamming. It wasn't as regimented as everybody thinks it was, with everybody coming in and everybody's got everything ready to do a session. There was nobody saying we had to do it this way or this way or this way. Somebody would say, "Let me hear a little bit of something." That would be the only leadership we would have out there.

Carl Perkins, bless his heart, he's a good friend of mine and always has been, but he's careful of what he says. He wants it to look like Sun was a smooth-running place. But this was not a smooth-running place, believe me. There were some knockdown, drag-out fights. Jerry Lee and I got into it one day and he just went off on me. He had me up against that wall and we were about to get into it because we had been here all night. We were tired and drunk and sobered up and got drunk again and sobered up again. We had been here since noon, one o'clock or so, and here it was about three or four o'clock in the morning and we haven't got nothing—haven't even got a cut on anything. That's the night the sermon went on out here.

The sermon Riley is referring to took place in early October 1957 while Lewis and band were trying to catch a keeper on "Great Balls of Fire." Arguing back and forth with all the conviction drunk men can summon when they believe something is right, Lewis and Phillips engage in a discourse on biblical interpretation, the evil in men, the evil in rock and roll, and, more specifically, the evil in "Great Balls of Fire." Phillips maintains his dignity throughout (although you can smell the irritation brewing), but Lewis draws on his early years spent at the Southwestern Bible Institute in east Texas, turning in a fiery, righteous sermon. It's an amazing performance, one that offers astonishing insight into the philosophical struggle and moral conflict that raged in Lewis's God-fearing, hell-raising soul. And it's topped only by the wicked, salacious run-through of "Great Balls of Fire" that followed, the one that would be released the next month as Sun No. 281.

What follows is a transcript of that sermon, which can be heard on Bear Family's boxed set, *Classic Jerry Lee Lewis*.

JERRY LEE LEWIS: H-E-L-L!
(UNKNOWN): Great God almighty, great balls of fire.
BILLY LEE RILEY: That's right!
LEWIS: It says make merry with the joy of God, but when it comes to worldly music, rock and roll . . .
RILEY: Rock it out!
LEWIS: . . . or anything that like, you have done brought yourself into the world and you're in the world and you hadn't

come from out of the world, and you're still a sinner. You're a sinner, and unless you be saved and born again, and be made as a little child and walk before God and be holy. And brother, I mean you got to be so pure, for no sin shall enter there. No sin! 'Cause it says "no sin." It don't say "just a little bit." It says "no sin shall enter there." Brother, not one little bit. You got to walk and talk with God to go to heaven. You've got to be so good that it's pitiful. Tellin' you what I know.

RILEY: Hallelujah!

SAM PHILLIPS: All right. Now look, Jerry, religious conviction doesn't mean anything resembling extremism. All right. You mean to tell me that you're gonna take the Bible, that you gonna take God's word, and that you gonna revolutionize the whole universe. Now listen, Jesus Christ was sent here by God o'mighty.

LEWIS: Right!

PHILLIPS: Did he convict? Did he save all of the people in the world?

LEWIS: No, but he *tried* to.

PHILLIPS: He sure did. Now wait just a minute. Jesus Christ came into this world. He tolerated man. He didn't preach from one pulpit. He went around and did good.

LEWIS: That's right. He preached everywhere. He preached all over the land. He preached on the water. He done everything. He healed!

PHILLIPS: Now here's the difference . . .

LEWIS: Are you following those that healed? Like Jesus Christ did? Well it's happening every day.

PHILLIPS: What do you mean?

LEWIS: The blinded eyes are open.

PHILLIPS: Jerry . . .

LEWIS: The lame were made to walk.

PHILLIPS: Jesus Christ . . .

LEWIS: The crippled were made to walk.

PHILLIPS: Jesus Christ, in my opinion, is just as real today as he was when he came into this world.

LEWIS: Right. Right. You're so right you don't know what you're saying about it.

PHILLIPS: Now then, I was saying [unintelligible]. Now listen, I'm telling you out of my heart, and I have studied the Bible a little bit . . .

LEWIS: Well, I have, too. I've studied it through and through and through and through and through. I know what I'm talking about.

PHILLIPS: Listen, when you think that you can't do good, to be a rock and roll exponent [unintelligible].

LEWIS: You can do good, Mr. Phillips, don't get me wrong.

PHILLIPS: Wait a minute, now, when I say do good . . .

LEWIS: You can have a kind heart . . .

PHILLIPS: I don't mean, I don't mean . . .

LEWIS: . . . you can help people . . .

PHILLIPS: You can save souls.

LEWIS: No, no, no. How can the devil save souls? What are you talkin' about? Man, I got the *devil* in me! If I didn't have, I'd be a Christian.

PHILLIPS: Well, you may have it . . .

LEWIS: Jesus, *heal* this man. He cast the devil out. The devil says, "Where can I go?" Says, "Can I go into this *swine*?" He says, "Yeah, go into him." Didn't it go into him?

PHILLIPS: Jerry, the point I'm trying to make is, if you believe what you're saying, you got no alternative whatsoever out of, listen, out of . . .

LEWIS: Mr. Phillips, it ain't what you believe. It's what's written in the Bible.

PHILLIPS: Well, wait a minute, now . . .

LEWIS: It's what's there, Mr. Phillips.

PHILLIPS: No, no, no . . .

LEWIS: It ain't what you believe, it's just what . . .

PHILLIPS: If it's not what you believe, then how do you interpret the Bible? Huh? How do you interpret the Bible if it's not what you believe?

LEWIS: Well, there's some people you just can't tell 'em, 'cause they [unintelligible].

RILEY: Let's cut it, man.

. . . . *RILEY* . . . .

Everybody was drinking that night. At one point I just got tired and said, "I'm leaving, man. I'm tired. I'm sick of this place, man, I'm leaving. I'm gone." And Jerry Lee said, "Well, you just go on, I'll get my mother to play guitar." So I said, innocently, "Well, you just get your mammy to do it," and he grabbed me and said, "Don't talk about my mother that way." There were a few words, but it was all right. I mean, we went on back out and tried something else and then everybody was just fine. And the next time we came in we did the session and it was fine. It would just get that way sometime.

It wasn't like everybody says, where you came in here and Sam was the big groomer or the big charmer. At first, Sam had a lot of us believing that he was the god of the record industry. Everybody was a little bit leery of him, and everybody except me was, "Yes sir, Mr. Phillips," but he and I were not like that. He and I fought. We'd holler at each other and scream at each other. We didn't like each other personally, but he knew what I had to offer and I knew that he was talented.

The difference with Jack was, Jack was one of us. He was a musician and a *good* musician. He understood. Sam was just a radio man. Jack

The eternal badass, Billy Lee Riley in 1994 (Trey Harrison)

122

could talk to us. We never really, I don't remember but one time when I got mad at Jack Clement, and that was right after he'd had a nose job. He went and had his nose cut down a little bit and he came in here and still had the bandages on it. We was doing a session and, I don't know, something happened. I was drinking real heavy and when I drank I was pretty wild. And something happened and I came into the control room and said, "You and I are about to go to Fist City," and he said, "No, my nose!" And everybody got tickled and it turned out to be a big joke.

But we could relate to Jack because he was on our level. Sam, we had him up here. He was the owner of all this. He was *big time*. He was put on a pedestal by a lot of people, but I've never put anybody on a pedestal and that's why he and I fought. I've never seen a superior person. Everybody was just another person to me. I met Elvis later, the sixties, and every time I was with Elvis I talked to him just like I'm talking to you and he liked it. That world he had, that's not what he wanted. He would have rather been able to be like me or you or anybody—go to a restaurant and eat and not have anybody bothering him. It all just happened to him too quick. He lived with it and accepted it, but he didn't like it.

I remember I did two shows for him, two of his private New Year's Eve shows. One was at the Thunderbird and one was at some other club. It was me, B. J. Thomas, and four other people playing. When it came my time to play, I went out onstage and I saw him and Priscilla sitting right in the front row, and I thought, "I wonder what he would do if I sang some of his songs?" The first one I did was "It's Now or Never," and he just went wild. He loved it to death, so I did several more. He liked it. It didn't make him feel bad. And another time I was on the set with him in Los Angeles on *Girls! Girls! Girls!*, and I didn't light his cigars for him and I didn't jump every time he hollered, you know, and I think he enjoyed that, because he didn't have any of that in his life.

But Sam liked that idea of being put up there and he expected that out of us. That's what Jerry Lee did, and so did Elvis. I'm not putting Sam down in no sense, but we just didn't jibe as much as Jack and I did. I enjoyed a session with Jack a lot more than I did a session with Sam. A lot of times Jack and I would be doing a good session and Sam would come in after he'd been out all night and drunk, and he'd come in wanting to show us how to do it and he'd screw it all up and everybody'd get uninterested until he left, and then we'd get back on the show.

Later on in the fifties, like in '58 and '59, Sam would rent the studio out if somebody wanted to do a session and Jack would be the engineer. And there was a group that came in here from Little Rock—very classy, classy people, real nice suits and ties. And they wanted to record their son, who was maybe eighteen or nineteen years old. They brought the whole family, neighbors, friends, all of them came in here in their nice, dressy clothes. We'd all been in the back, drinking during the breaks, and about halfway through the session, Jack—he was drinking, too—he decided he wanted a banjo on the song. I'd never had a banjo in my hands in my life, but we tuned it like a guitar so I could at least make a chord on it. So I was sitting out there playing that banjo and all of a sudden that Thunderbird wine hit me like a ton of lead, and I fell completely off that stool, banjo and all, right on my butt. Those people didn't know what was going on.

And that same night, before that happened, Sam had come down to the studio. He had been out on Coral Lake—him and Jerry Lee—and he was about as drunk as I was, and he just barged in the front door during the session and said, "What's going on here?" He looked over at J.M.'s empty drum cases and he opened the top of that bass-drum case, curled up in there and pulled the top on over it. We just looked at those people and said, "He owns this studio."

I have to give him some credit, though. "Red Hot" came out after Sam played me the record he cut on Billy "The Kid"

Emerson. Of course, it was a slow thing, but we went out and completely changed it. "Flying Saucer Rock and Roll" was brought to me by him. And I got to give Sam credit on that, too. He did engineer that and he did help us put that together and make it happen like it did. He heard something we wasn't hearing. He wanted it to be spacy, and Sam said to Roland, "Play me something that sounds like spacemen, like something coming out of Mars." So Roland came up with that little lick at the beginning and Sam just loved it. He really loved it. When we finished it, he said, "Man, that's great. That's got to be a hit." And it should've been.

. . . . *J A N E S* . . . .

Riley was really searching for a style and the closest he ever came to a style, in my opinion, was on the first three or four records he had, like "Flying Saucer Rock and Roll" and "Red Hot." After that he kind of changed his style. Riley couldn't decide if he wanted to do blues or rock and roll. I guess he wanted to do it all.

Sometimes it's hard to come up with the right material and sometimes it's the direction someone may be trying to take you. It's not always the artist's fault. Riley always had a patience problem. He's been on several labels and tried several different things. Probably, maybe Riley needed to be produced by someone who really understood him, because he is a great talent. He's a great idea person. I think when we had our original band together, had we stuck together as a band and kept trying the direction we were headed in, it was just a matter of time before we had a smash hit.

And too, it was difficult then. Sam would maybe release four or five artists at once and sometimes you'd kind of get lost in the shuffle. Not due to anyone's fault, it's just the radio stations and the distributors could only handle so many records from a particular label and get the proper exposure for them. Riley may have been a victim of that on a couple of occasions, too. It's a shame. There were a lot of people back then that probably should've had hit records, but you've got to understand, man, Sun Records at the time I came onboard was a two-person operation, and then later they added a third person and later a fourth and like that. It was a small company. It wasn't like a big label. They had big-label success, but they just didn't have the personnel. We got an enormous number of records played that probably other labels couldn't have, and we'd have regional things on artists that maybe should've been national. But when you've got Carl Perkins, Jerry Lee Lewis, and Johnny Cash all going out at the same time and you throw a couple other records in there with it, it's easy to get lost in the shuffle.

When Sam started Phillips International, right out of the box we had "Lonely Weekends" and "Raunchy" and several other chart records. We definitely had a unique sound in the studio there and combination of musicians and everybody. But we weren't the whole business. They had to make room for some of the other folks, too. Hayden Thompson was a good artist. We had one particular record on Hayden, "Love My Baby," and Jerry Lee played on that along with me and Van Eaton. That could've been a hit record at that time.

Back then Sonny Burgess had one of the best show bands that you'll ever see in your life. They had a seven-piece band and put on one of the best shows you'll ever see by anybody. And I thought they had a good record, but I think they were much better in person than they were on their records. But timing is everything. If you walk across the street one second you get across fine and everything's fine. You try it again five seconds later and a bus runs over you. You have to acknowledge that and think about that. Timing is everything and sometimes it's just not in the cards at that particular time. There's no point in crying about it. Be thankful that you had the opportunity. I think all of them are. I just think there's some frustration here and there. And I think they recognize in their heart that probably nobody else in the world would've worked with them at that time because they were raw. We were all raw, but Sam had seen potential in us.

Sam would sometimes put records out on artists and he *knew* that he didn't have the record at the time, but he didn't want to keep stringing them along. He wanted to give them a little hope while he searched for that right thing, you know? There were a lot of records that were released that probably shouldn't have been released, and I think that was behind a lot of it. But you know, there's only so much one person can do. History has proven that he's done his share.

The man that did it all was Sam. Without Sam there wouldn't have been any of those guys. I would've never had an opportunity to do it and a lot of other people wouldn't have, either. Sam is someone that, he's gotten a lot of recognition, but you stop and think about the people he got started in the business. He's amazing. I'm talking about the musicians and engineers and producers, not to mention the great artists. He had an ear like nobody in the world. I think the most important thing I learned from being around Sam was, the thing I was most amazed by, was his ability to handle people, to get the most out of people, to put people at ease and get the most out of them. And the fact that he was strictly his own man, he was not afraid. When he had it right, he knew it. I remember one time I told him, "Mr. Phillips, I made a mistake in that," and he said, "Don't worry about it. The *feel*," he says, "it's got the *feel*. That's the cut I want." And I'm not going to tell you which record it was, but over the years I've never had someone come up to me and say, "Hey man, you made a mistake on that record." I've heard people say, "Man, that was a great record," so the man knew what the hell he was talking about.

He didn't let a little minor mistake mess up a perfect cut, and I've seen people do that in the studio time and time again. Screw up a good take just for the sake of some technicality that didn't mean a damn thing. Going in and erasing the track and redoing it with something that never turned out as good as what you already had. You've got to know when you've got it right and when to stop, and that seems to be one of the big problems today. People don't have enough confidence in themselves to say, "That's it." And Sam was never afraid of that. He knew what he wanted and he had his convictions and he stuck to them come hell or high water, and I haven't seen no one prove him wrong yet.

. . . . Y E L V I N G T O N . . . .

Sam was everything back then. The producer, the engineer, he set up all the mikes. He did it all. Sam was good to work for. He was real pleasant and was very straightforward. He'd tell you what he liked and didn't like. He didn't hem and haw about it. He never really got on anybody—not any of us, anyway. He was a real nice-looking man. Had coal-black hair and piercing eyes, you know? He had thick eyebrows and he could furrow them things and look real menacing. He could be intimidating. I remember I would "yes sir" and "no sir" him because I thought he was older than me. Come to find out, though, I'm five years older than Sam.

0

"Fluke" is the perfect nickname for W. S. Holland, for that's pretty much how he describes the key events in his early career—a career that placed him behind the drum kit for the duration of Carl Perkins's time at Sun as well as the handful of sides recorded there by fellow Jackson native Carl Mann. (He also brought his unique, effortlessly swinging drum style to the bulk of Johnny Cash's Columbia recordings in the 1960s and 1970s, including the landmark live set *At Folsom Prison*.) When pressed to explain the intricacies of his art— the details of a session or how a good honky-tonk group can blossom into an incredible rockabilly unit—the normally gregarious and talkative man demurs. (Maybe he's saving it all for the autobiography he's hoping someday to write.)

What he will tell you, though, is that it all just happened, that he and every-one else at Sun were simply doing the only thing they knew how to do.

. . . . W . S . H O L L A N D . . . .

It didn't feel like we were doing anything different at Sun, and I didn't have any idea that that's what we would be doing. That was in '54, so I was nineteen then. I was working at a place here in Jackson in the air conditioning and refrigeration business, and I worked there another year after we went to Sun because nothing was certain. When we first started, we didn't think we were going to be doing anything that anybody else wasn't already doing. I sure didn't think that I was going to do that for a living. It didn't even enter my mind.

29

At that time we didn't really know what we were doing was so different. Later, we did, when we began to learn more about the business. Our first time there, we went into Sun Records, set up our instruments in the middle of the floor, just like setting up in your living room. There wasn't anything to the place. Then Sam came in and introduced himself to Carl, Clayton, J.D., and myself, and we talked for a while and he went on into the control room and said, "Well, let's play something so I can hear what you sound like." What's interesting—or weird—now, looking back on it, looking at the room, there were no baffles or separators. There was one mike for the whole drum set and a mike for the bass and a mike for the gui-tar and amplifier, just sitting out in the middle of the floor. Everything was bleeding through all the mikes. And really, if you look back at it now, there was really not a lot of recording equipment there. But that's what made it so real, and that's what I've always liked—and still do to this day. I like to go into the studio and when we leave, the record is made. That's what we would do at Sun, and that's what was so unique about it.

Sam would just let the tape roll. That's what the Million-Dollar Quartet session was. We were in there for a recording session and some guys just dropped by—Elvis, Johnny Cash, and the guys—and Sam just had the machine on. I didn't really know it. I don't know if anybody knew it. That's one reason that I guess the sound wasn't all that great. But there was a unique way of doing things back then and I still like it today better than how it is now. It makes the music sound more real than the way it does today. And Sam would do things that I don't know if he really knew what he was doing or not. But I don't know if *any* of us knew what we were doing. We were just doing the only thing we could do. I've talked to a lot of guys nowadays and they say, "We're going into the studio at this time and we're gonna do it this way and play something that-a-way." And that's the difference from when we started. We couldn't do that. We could do what we did and that's all we knew to do. I think it was the same way with Sam. He knew to do what he was doing and that's the reason the records came off so real-sounding. I know he would do things like, we cut a song called "Your True Love." And it was too slow, and instead of redoing it like maybe we should've done, or like we'd have done today, Sam just speeded it up with the machine, where it didn't change the sound of the music all that much. Of course, it made Carl sound like a borderline Donald Duck. That's what made Sun Records what it is today, unique stuff like that.

I've said many times that I don't think anybody in the studio, including Sam, really knew what they were doing. But it worked. As far as anybody saying, "Hey, let's do it this way. We could do it that way, but if we do it this way we could get a hit," I don't think anybody . . . I don't know what they do today. I don't know that record producers today actually know what's going to be a hit. Everybody's just trying things. It seems to me that if somebody knew what a hit record was going to be, they'd be releasing one every two hours.

Even that thing I did with Carl Mann, "Mona Lisa," that was something where we went in, Sam heard it and liked it, and he just turned on the machine. The way that came about, my wife Joyce and I visited a little club south of Jackson called the Cotton Bowl, and there was a band onstage. Never met any of them before, except one guy, Jimmy Martin, who was playing drums. They had this boy that was singing, and he was doing those Nat King Cole songs like that. Jumped up-like. So I met him after the show, thinking, "This is something different," and we became friends. Then Carl and myself and a boy named Eddie Bush, a guitarist, and the bass player Wee Willie Stevenson got together and did some stuff, "Mona Lisa," and I took them over to introduce them to Sam, and he liked what we were doing and we got a recording contract. I don't know who can take credit for that arrangement. I could say it was me or I could say we all did it together, but really it was just one of those things that happened.

And that's what was so great about doing stuff at Sun. I don't think there was a clock in the building. I remember going in at noon, we'd leave Jackson and get to the studio at noon, maybe one o'clock, and some mornings, it would be getting light when we would walk out of the studio the next morning. There was a time when we didn't realize what a session actually was. We didn't go by a three-hour session or a clock, and I liked that. Still do. The worst thing in the world in a studio is a clock. If you've got to worry about hurrying up to get through, you're gonna mess something up, goof up something.

I learned different things after I left Sun. I know now that the time's got to be right and the session's got to be done and you have to file your union forms and everything's got to be done just right. But if you got a studio booked for six hours and you're into it five hours and forty-five minutes, but you're two hours from being through, it takes a lot out of it for me. But you look back at those old days, it's unbelievable how it was done then in comparison to how it is today.

For example, Larry Butler, who is my all-time favorite record producer, he's in Nashville, played piano with us some. Larry's

Jim Dickinson, hearing strange noises that others let pass by (Trey Harrison)

the type guy that he can hear a song before it's ever recorded. He can hear the finished product in his head. He can get a group of musicians, a studio, an engineer, and then go into the studio and he can make that record like building a house. You can visualize what a house is going to look like before you build it, and when you're through with it, it's like, "Hey, that's what I saw." Larry Butler can do that.

But that wasn't what happened back then. Nobody back in the Sun Records days ever did that—not Sam, not Jack. Nobody. It was not something that somebody heard. Like, "I hear this in my head, now let's cut it and get it to sound like it did in my head." It didn't happen. Everybody was just doing what they knew how to do and that's the way it came off. It's a weird thing to even think about.

. . . . *JANES* . . . .

The only thing we knew we were doing was having fun. We had a lot of fun. We really enjoyed what we were doing, and we were thankful for the opportunity to do it because it just wasn't a thing you got to do right then. There wasn't that much recording or that much opportunity available, so we really enjoyed what we were doing. It was a fun thing. It wasn't a toiling work thing at all. I grew up in St. Louis and there were probably a couple of studios there but it was strictly for the elite—the jingles and that kind of thing. But a guy like me probably wouldn't even be allowed in the studio. And Nashville had a lot of recording going on but it was pretty controlled even at that point. They just used certain people.

The records we cut then, we had to do it right because we were recording mono, and if we did make a mistake, if it wasn't too bad and it didn't take away from the record, you'd just let it stay in there. It didn't make any difference. In a session, maybe you take five takes on a song and four of them are real good, but that one take, it captures the moment. And they felt good. You could listen to a record and tell that the musicians and the singer and all the performers on that record were really trying, that they were really enjoying themselves. You could tell that people really enjoyed what they were doing. I know I certainly was, and everybody that I was associated with was.

. . . . JIM DICKINSON . . . .
The studio is where it started making sense for me. I didn't take playing live seriously until folk music started to happen, and folk music was so easy that I couldn't not do it. Plus, it was more of what I was interested in—I've always been interested in primitive music, primitive culture. Although the rock and roll my band played was plenty primitive, folk music was more appealing to me.

When I came back to Memphis, folk music was just about to happen and the coffeehouse scene was just starting up and, again, it was so easy that I just fell into it. But when I started working in the studio, which was almost right away—I guess in '62 or '63 I started doing studio work—that made sense to me. See, the audience has never appealed to me. I hear musicians tell me all the time that they feel this charge come back from the audience. Well, I don't feel anything from the audience. I'm more aware of the audience when I'm in the studio than when I'm onstage. The studio is still a live performance. When you're making a record, why do they call it a record? Because it's something you can't repeat! You go back to the example that everybody uses in the blues, Robert Johnson—I doubt if Robert Johnson was very thrilling to see performing live. How could it have been? But I think a lot of primitive musicians intuitively understand the recording process. Johnson certainly was one of them. And I've experienced it as a producer: People come along who just understand what's going on. And it's a mystery; what happens in the studio is a mystery, and a lot of people don't get it. That's why you have to have a producer. But every once in a while you get somebody, like Elvis, who understands about the microphone and projects themselves—the soul of the moment, if you will—into the microphone, the way they are feeling in their soul at the moment into the microphone. That's where good records come from, and there's something about Memphis and the recording process here as well, because I've recorded not all over the world but a lot of damn places and there's just something about Memphis and the recording process. People come here and feel it.

It was the "My Babe" session with the Jesters where I first looked into Sam's eyes and saw the thing. His eyes are black. They aren't brown. But you realize when you look at the guy that this is the way he looked at Elvis, this is the way he looked at Howlin' Wolf. You see these whirling pools of insanity and you believe you can do something more than what you can. He totally had it, totally had it. Still has it. Could do it now if he wanted. Knox and I back in the seventies put together a deal for Sam to produce a B. B. King record. It would've been at the time a significant record, and it never crossed our minds that he wouldn't do it, you know? We had it literally all set to go. Knox went to Sam and asked him about it, and Sam said no. And I said, "Why, Knox? Did he give you a reason?" He said, "Yeah, he said, 'You just can't go to Picasso and ask him to paint one little picture.'" That's the way he looks at it.

There are people who will say about Sam's period of genius that it's a ten-year period of time, and it is the same period of time as his alcoholism, and also it's right after his shock-treatment therapy, which is supposed to last ten years. *[Phillips underwent electroshock treatments in 1951 for "nervous exhaustion."]* And I know he has a fascination with high voltage. I saw him at the old Sounds of Memphis studio; it was a temporary location and it was wired up all phony. It had been haywired. And they were having some kind of fuse problem and Sam popped open the fuse box and took a screwdriver and laid it across four fuses, holding the metal part. It looked like lightning struck the thing. And Sam has yet to even recoil. He says, "A little one-ten doesn't hurt you. You need two-twenty every now and then just to *know you're alive.*" He's not the average human being by any stretch of the imagination.

A forgotten name by all but the most obsessive Sun aficionados, Rayburn Anthony was a singer from Jackson, Tennessee, who spent much of the 1950s doing club shows in a band with W. S. Holland and Carl Mann. He cut two sessions at Sun—one in the old building, the other in the new place on Madison Avenue—and had a pair of singles issued on the label. But neither 1959's "Alice Blue Gown" (more noteworthy for the flip side cover of "St. Louis Blues") nor 1960's "Who's Gonna Shoe Your Pretty Feet" gave Phillips much reason to summon Anthony back to the studio for a third crack at a hit.

. . . . . . R A Y B U R N   A N T H O N Y . . . . . .
Me and Carl Mann and W. S. Holland are all from the same area, around Jackson. We used to play in this place called Pine Ridge, just a little south of Jackson, but they used to drive over to Memphis all the time to record at Sun. So one time W.S. asked

if I would go down there with them and sing a couple of songs for Sam Phillips, to see if he was interested in me. So I did. I went down there with them and Eddie Bush—just piled in the car and went down there, didn't make an appointment or anything. We just left. But Sam was there, so we went into the studio and Sam asked me if I would go out there by myself and sing a couple songs without anybody playing. We'd planned on W.S. to play drums and have Eddie on guitar, but he wanted me to just sing by myself, so I did. And he came out and he said he'd like to do a record on me. That's how it started.

It hadn't been any big dream of mine to be on Sun. I really wanted to record, but everybody that sings wants to record, I guess. I knew about Carl Perkins and everybody coming down to Sun, so I wanted to go down there too, but it didn't make a lot of difference. There was another label there that was doing pretty well at the time, Hi Records, and I was going to check them out if Phillips didn't like me. But after I sang he came out and said, "Hey, that's great. Let's do a deal," so I went back and recorded the next week. We had Eddie Bush on guitar, W.S. on drums, and Wee Willie Stevenson on bass. We cut some stuff and I think about ten days later he had the records pressed up. Of course, they didn't sell.

Exactly what happened with it was, we did a version of "St. Louis Blues," because back then the trend was to redo an older song in a new, rock style. Like Carl Mann did with "Mona Lisa." We did that with "St. Louis Blues" and it turned out pretty good. So Sam mailed out the records and our plan was for me to go to St. Louis to start my promotional tour there, and he had several other places lined up for me to go. But two weeks before it was set to be released, the whole thing about payola came out, and my tour was canceled. Then the record just kind of withered away. I think about everything at that time died for a while.

The sessions went pretty good. If it had been any looser there you'd of gone to sleep. It wasn't like recording sessions now.

Now, if you go to Nashville you've got a ten o'clock and a two o'clock and a six o'clock and you go in and work three hours and take an hour break, and of course everybody's there to do the song. But at Sun you just went out and did the song and if you didn't like the take, you'd do it again, and if you still did not like it, you just kind of wandered off and came back later and did it again. There was no pressure there. You'd drive down there at maybe seven o'clock at night to start the session. The guy that played bass for us, Wee Willie Stevenson, worked at the Coke company in Jackson driving a truck. So we would go pick him up after he'd get off work, leave Jackson at about seven. We'd get to Sun at eight and we'd plan on doing a session at ten or eleven. And Stevenson had to go back to work the next morning at six, and sometimes we'd bring him back from the studio and let him off at work, straight from the studio. And of course the next night he would call and say he hated me and he hated Sam Phillips because he was so tired.

I liked Sam Phillips and I think he liked me. I really think he thought he could get a hit record on me, but I think he was concentrating on other things. They had just moved into the new studio, between the first time I recorded and the second time. That took up a lot of his time. The new place was okay, but you know how it is when you move. The new studio seemed colder, but it was a nice studio, and the sound was just great. Much better than the old, but that was what you were used to, you know? It was just so different at the time. Everything was so raw. You could go in there right now and cut the same thing and you would not get the same sound, under no circumstances.

If Rayburn Anthony didn't exactly earn a place in the pantheon of Sun Records, he at least got a couple of shots at it. Michigan singer Johnny Pavlick (who'd had some minor regional hits under the name Johnny Powers) had only one chance to get it right at Sun, and by his own admission he damn near blew it. Sales-wise, Powers didn't set the rockabilly woods afire, but he managed at least to pop out a fine single that, nearly thirty years after its release, has made him a revered cult figure among fanatics in the United States and abroad. And for good reason: Both "With Your Love, With Your Kiss" and "Be Mine, All Mine," the plug and flip sides of his 1959 Sun release, rank among the label's best one-shot offerings. The former is a somewhat raucous ballad that finds a middle ground between honky-tonk and doo-wop, with a full-throttle vocal and echo-laden machine-gun drums from J. M. Van Eaton. On the flip, Powers does his best leering Elvis amid a driving acoustic guitar (compliments of Brad Suggs) and a fine sax break from Martin Willis. Powers sounds like a sneering badass on both cuts, but he claims he was anything but during his one nocturnal session at the studio.

. . . . J O H N N Y   P O W E R S . . . .

I came from a musical family—a Polish family. On my dad's side they were all musicians, and my dad played banjo. As a young kid I was always exposed to the oom-pah bands on the weekends. Then I got into listening to Lonnie Baron, who was a country artist up near Detroit who lived in Richmond, Michigan. There was a guy named Marvin Maynard who came up from West Virginia and lived one street over from where I lived in Utica. I was just a kid when I met him. He played guitar, so naturally I got turned on by the guitar and bought one myself. He showed me how

Portrait of the artist as a young greaser: a late-fifties shot of Michigan rockabilly Johnny Powers (Courtesy Norton Records)

to play the chords and from that point I picked up pretty easy on it, and awhile later I went to work for Jimmy Williams and the Drifters. I guess I was about fifteen or sixteen at the time. I was just playing rhythm guitar. I would go around and watch all these country artists—Casey Clark, who used to bring in a lot of Nashville acts, and, of course, Lonnie Baron. I would listen to him on the radio and play guitar along with it.

So then I started working at this place called Bill's Barn. It was a barn that had a nice floor and a pot-bellied stove, and it was a hangout for the weekend. I played there for a number of years and then cut a record. See, in 1957 Jack Scott, a local guy, came out with a song called "My Baby She's Gone" on ABC-Paramount, and my guitar player, Stan Getz, played bass on all of Jack's records, and I kind of liked that sound and kind of idolized Jack a little bit. I thought, "I'm going to cut me a record and see what happens." So I went down to Fortune Records and recorded "Honey Let's Go to the Rock and Roll Show" and "Your Love." It came out, but back then you never knew how the singles did because you didn't know the sales of anything, but I don't think it was a big hit record. It did get a lot of airplay, at least in the Midwest. I don't know how it did outside of that. Fair, I guess. Then George Braxton at Fox Records approached me to do a session, so I took Stan and the rest of the guys to the studio and we recorded "Long Blond Hair" and "Rock Rock." That single went to number 3 in Seattle and charted in different areas, but the label was so small nothing really happened. Nowadays, just about every rockabilly band in the world has played "Long Blond Hair."

After Fox Records, Sun came along. It was kind of a weird situation how that came about. There was a guy named Don Zee, who used to be a pretty famous DJ here in Detroit. My manager at the time was Tommy Moore, and he took me to Don Zee, who had a little recording studio in Utica—just a recorder and a makeshift engineer board. I went in there with a group called the Paragons and cut a tape of a bunch of songs.

My manager's mother-in-law lived in Montgomery, Alabama, so he went down to see her and took this tape with him. While he was there he happened to go on the air at some radio station in Montgomery and played the tape. The disc jockey's phones just lit up, and from that he guessed he could get to Sam Phillips, so he called Sam, and Tommy and Don Zee met him at Sun and struck some kind of deal, then they called me. I had no idea any of this was going on.

I knew about Sun. A friend of mine named Ray Mallett went down there to audition. He was a good singer but came back disappointed and started looking for some other kind of work. But I thought if he couldn't get a deal with Sun Records, I never would. I wouldn't have even tried it. See, Sun Records was a dream for almost every artist of that era. It was a label that would be a dream for almost anybody to be on. Not just because of Elvis and the other people involved with it—Carl Perkins and everybody else—but because the sound they were getting was so unique for that era. The echo and the quality of the recordings. I mean they *rocked*. There were a lot of rock and roll things out there then, but nothing that rocked like the Sun Records stuff. You listen to them today and they sound kind of thin compared to today's rock, but they had that echo that was so unique. That slapback echo. And I think there was a kind of freedom Sam gave his artists and musicians. Of course, I'm sure he gave them some guidelines, helping them. Sam was the engineer on most of the stuff I did.

It was the latter part of '58 when I went down there. I can't remember the month, but I can remember one thing—I was nervous, man. I look back at it, my voice back then when I was singing over there, I was at my weakest point because of the nerves. I don't think I gave myself the opportunity that I had in my hand—I didn't use it because I was walking into the studio and thinking, "Elvis was here and Carl Perkins was here," and I'm wondering, "Is this the place where Elvis stood? Is this the mike that he used?" You know, it's *Sam Phillips!* I mean, come on. When I was singing back then, I had a lot of guts and power and stuff, but when I walked in there I lost every bit of that. I mean, sheesh, it was, "Pinch me, I'm dreaming. This must be a dream." I listen to the recordings today and I think, "Boy, I wish I had been paying attention to what I was doing instead of being a fan or a groupie."

Just walking in there—I think it had a certain amount of electricity for everyone who walked in there. I know what I felt, and the sound of that studio was just amazing. About five years ago I was down there doing some demos with a band called Reverend Horton Heat, and it still has that sound. That room—the way the acoustics are in that room I don't think could ever be duplicated. You could put a drum kit anywhere in that room and you wouldn't have to use baffles to isolate the drums. The walls absorb that sound and you can just catch it right there with a microphone. It's kind of strange, but it was a great feeling. It's very hard to explain, because I think everybody has their own feeling about when they first walked in there, but I think it was the electricity that came out of that place just got everybody.

When I walked in there, I was so out of it I didn't know who was there at the time. I just saw musicians. Didn't know who they were or what their names were. Sam was in the control room and these guys were sitting in the studio. I was on one side of the room and they were on the other side. Charlie Rich sitting behind the piano? I didn't know who he was. I just knew it was a piano player sitting there. I found that out after I got back home. And James Van Eaton, Jerry Lee Lewis's drummer? I called him Whitey, because he had kind of blondish hair. I didn't know what his name was.

Sam and Jack Clement were in the control room, and Clement just talked to me over the microphone, said, "Here's the next song," and I'd run it down and we'd go over and over and over it, and finally my voice started running out. Remember, I got off the airplane that day, got to the hotel, relaxed a little bit, then went to the studio and recorded—bang, bang, bang, bang. It was an evening, maybe late-afternoon session. I signed the contract, did the session, did everything all at one time. On some of the songs, like "Me and My Rhythm Guitar," you can hear my voice is giving out.

After the session, I went back home, started playing again at Bill's Barn and hanging out like a teenager. The record came out in 1959 and it felt great. I had a bit of smartness to myself. You know, imagine being single and walking around the girls saying, "I've got a record on Sun," and bragging to your musician friends and so forth.

But Sun Records started unwinding, I guess. It had reached its peak. The music started changing and for whatever reason Sam either got tired of it or just felt like it was time for things to go to sleep. I didn't know what was going on then, but as I look back on it, you had doo-wop coming in strong, and you also had everybody leaving Sun. Carl Perkins left, Johnny Cash took a walk, so it was disappointing, I'm sure. But Sun Records was the granddaddy of things happening back then. There were a lot of independent labels, but Sun stood out above all of them. I guess the only other one was Motown, and I'm the only artist on the planet that has recorded for Sun Records and Motown Records, the two most historic independent labels ever.

SIX

Sunset

If the Jesters' "Cadillac Man" had been the last single issued on Sun, it would've provided the label with a fiercely rocking sendoff. Unfortunately it remains one of only a handful of really worthwhile tracks cut at Sam Phillips's new digs in Memphis at 639 Madison Avenue, which opened in 1960. Although the studio was a just a few blocks east of its former location at 706 Union Avenue, more than distance separated the two structures.

The move made sense for many practical reasons. The control room at 706 was too small to house the new equipment Sun needed to stay competitive in the 1960s. Phillips had also been toying with the idea of renting his studio to outside artists and, its history notwithstanding, the old place didn't offer much for newcomers in search of multitrack technology and other accoutrements. Besides, the building on Union couldn't contain the growing number of staffers at the label. Sun was clearly in need of a new home.

What it got was a lavishly appointed, state-of-the-art facility with a recording area about twice the size of the original studio, offices for everyone (plus a wet bar and jukebox in the boss's), and live echo chambers that—in theory, at least—rendered obsolete Phillips's reliable but archaic slapback tape method. Construction began in 1958; in a little more than a year the studio was being used to add overdubbed flourishes to Charlie Rich's breakthrough hit "Lonely Weekends," the basic track of which had been cut earlier at 706. The Sun production roster was beefed up with the addition of Scotty Moore, Bill Fitzgerald, Cecil Scaife, and Charles Underwood (the man who wrote Warren Smith's "Ubangi Stomp"), as well as Phillips's son Knox and, later, Roland Janes. By September 1960 the studio was opened officially amid much promotional hoopla, but its christening also signaled the end of Phillips's full-time involvement in his revamped enterprise.

It's tempting to read great import into Phillips's withdrawal from both production and hands-on operations at Sun. Wrongheaded theorists who believe rock and roll was dormant in the sixties until the arrival of the Beatles have even seen his inactivity as a statement of disdain and distaste for rock and roll's new direction. Certainly his productions from the fifties have little in common with the fussy, sometimes lavish creations of Berry Gordy and Phil Spector, the two producers who best defined the sound of the rock era Phillips chose to sit out.

Most likely, Phillips was simply burned out—disillusioned by countless failures, aware of the slim chance his relatively small enterprise had in the industry that pop music had suddenly become. Of the three artists Phillips thought would equal his success with Elvis Presley, Carl Perkins and Johnny Cash had left Sun for the big money offered by Columbia, and Jerry Lee Lewis had yet to recover from the 1958 hoo-ha following the news of his marriage to Myra Gale Brown, his thirteen-year-old cousin. (Jerry Lee would leave the label in 1963 to sign with Mercury, where he forged a straight-country sound that was almost as singular, and just as impassioned, as his vintage rock and roll style.) A marked decline in quality at the label followed the move to new quarters, with treacly pop pretty boys like Tony Rossini replacing the red-hot rockabillies. No wonder, then, that Phillips threw more time, money, and attention into building a Southern radio-station empire, no doubt a sounder investment of both money and emotion than an independent record label on its way to extinction.

The fact remains, however, that Phillips was unable (or if you want to be charitable, unwilling) to adapt to the changes in popular music—not just in rock and roll, but also in rhythm and blues, a more grievous failing considering

Phillips's long-standing love for the music and the overwhelming quality of his blues and vocal-group work during the infancy of the Memphis Recording Service. But he never lost the ability to cut amazing gutbucket blues records. Witness the 1962 recordings by Frank Frost issued that year on Sun's Phillips International subsidiary. A fine set of raw Mississippi juke-joint blues, the *Hey, Boss Man!* album arrived at the cusp of an R&B's mutation into soul. Considering that the mutation was taking place in Memphis, at Jim Stewart and Estelle Axton's Satellite studio, it's surprising that Phillips would opt to ignore those changes and work instead with an artist whose music—great as it was—represented several big steps backward.

Nevertheless, when Phillips fortified the production staff at the new quarters, he chose some of the men who had helped build his legacy. Roland Janes returned in the mid-seventies following the dissolution of his Sonic studio and a brief stint as a recording instructor at a Memphis vocational school. Scotty Moore hooked up again with Phillips a couple of years after his late-fifties split with Elvis.

145

. . . .*SCOTTY MOORE*. . . . .

When Elvis went in the army I started working with Slim Wallace, who had a little garage studio called Fernwood. There wasn't any money involved, but it was something to do, more or less. So we cut a record on Thomas Wayne in 1959, "Tragedy." It was a big one. Then we formed a corporation and started the whole business. We built a studio down on North Main in Memphis. We kept cutting records on Thomas and two or three other guys and finally spent all the money we'd made on the first one. I decided then that I was going to have to do something else. It was about that time that Sam was building his new studio, so I went by to see him and see how it was coming along. He offered me a job as production manager, so I bailed out of Fernwood and went to work for him. I was there for a while, and when Sam bought out a studio in Nashville— I'd say in about '64—I would go back and forth to both of them.

The studio in Nashville was downtown in a Masonic lodge-building. It was a three-story building. Huge place. The studio was up on the third floor. Rent was cheap because it was just wasted space for the lodge. Then it was tore down later and a big insurance building went in there. The people that put in the studio originally already had Billy Sherrill working with them. There weren't too many records cut there. I think Jerry Lee went up there and cut a couple. Things were happening more in Nashville than in Memphis at that time, and Sam wasn't averse to trying something different. It didn't work out, though, and Fred Foster at Monument bought Sam out.

I think with the new studio on Madison, Sam just wanted a bigger, better facility. The place over on Union was small and they didn't have much equipment. And he had been renting the old place. It was a larger studio and more modern equipment. That's basically it. They had offices. He didn't really have an office in the old place. He had a desk back in the back end of it, but it was mostly a storeroom. He replaced everything with new equipment. Sam built two different echo chambers there—live chambers. Before that he used the tape slap at the old place.

I guess it was better just because of the space alone. You had a lunchroom and a bar and a patio up on the roof. At the old place you had a little front office, and if there were too many people in there, some of them would have to stand out on the sidewalk.

I didn't play on more than just a few records at the new studio. I don't even recall who they were by. I produced some. I did a couple of songs on Jerry Lee and even brought Thomas Wayne over there after the Fernwood thing and cut a few records. A lot of the people I just knew from them coming in the studio. They were there for three or four hours and I might not ever see them again.

Before he rejoined the Phillips staff officially in 1974, Janes worked on many of the sessions cut at the Madison studio, including the final two dates by Jerry Lee Lewis in August 1963. The differences between the two studios, he says, were considerable.

. . . . R O L A N D   J A N E S . . . .

Paul Burlison was doing a session on Rocky Burnette and he called me and asked me if I wanted to play on it. I said, "Paul, I'm really rusty, I haven't played in a while," and he said, "Come on down anyway." So I came down and we did the album. In the process of being there I first did some independent work, and Knox, Sam's son, said he wanted me to go on salary, so I did. It was no problem.

It was as unique as the old studio. The old studio, the way Sam did the room was real unique, but it was just a rented building. Sam came [to the new studio] and incorporated a lot of his ideas. And it was strictly state-of-the-art at the time it was created. It felt a little strange, though, because we were really comfortable in the old studio. At the new place it seemed like everybody was on a little higher level intellectually. I don't know. It just didn't feel exactly right at that time. I think people had great expectations there and felt like we had stepped up to another level, and probably we had. But I don't know that we *wanted* to step up to the next level. I think we were doing pretty good where we were, you know?

There were more people there. He had hired a couple more girls upstairs and they had a promotion man and different things that we didn't have at the old studio. Everybody knew everybody, so it wasn't a thing like that. Nobody was mad at anybody. It's kind of like you're used to eating at McDonald's and all of a sudden you have to go to the Ritz. You're not real comfortable at the Ritz.

It was a totally different sound. I think it was probably cleaner, and you had more room and everything. We had a first-class live echo chamber here—we didn't have an echo chamber at the old studio. Sam's echo there was strictly a slapback echo. You could cut records that sounded more like the Nashville country things here than you could at the old studio. At first they had a few problems until they got the sound effects down just right—the room and the acoustics. It was a trial-and-error thing, sort of. At first we didn't have carpet on the floor and then finally we did, and that helped. It was just a matter of getting it fine-tuned. But it's a great room. It was great then and it's still a great room.

There was just a magic feeling [at the old studio]. First of all, you walked in the door and you knew everybody. If they were between takes you'd go right out from the office into the studio and then walk through the studio and up into the control room. It was a family thing. Everybody was involved—there weren't any prima donnas or anything like that. It was just a certain feel. And too, I think it was all new to us at that time. None of us had ever cut a hit record, so there was a lot of excitement.

. . . . M O O R E . . . .

At the old place, everybody says there was magic there. There wasn't any magic in there. It was just four walls. The magic was in the talent that came in, with Orbison, Cash, Perkins, all those folks. They created magic on record, but that doesn't mean the room is anything more than just a room. It was what happened in the room. When Carl and I went down there and did most of the cuts on that CD we did in '92 [706 ReUnion—A Sentimental Journey], we sat there and I asked Carl, I said, "Where's all that magic around here?" He laughed and said, "There ain't no damn magic in here. You know that."

It was nice being there and reminiscing, which basically was what that CD was all about. We had a lot of fun doing it. It was just old friends getting together and having a good time. But we could've done it anywhere. In fact, it ended up that we did a couple things up at Carl's house, in his den. I took a remote truck over there. With today's equipment you can do things like that. You can go out under a tree and cut a record.

Moore is probably right, and the proof of it is that a few men managed to find some magic in Sun's sterile new quarters, none more than Charlie Rich, a native of Forrest City, Arkansas, who embodied everything Sam Phillips said he was looking for in the days before Elvis Presley happened by 706. Not just one of the finest white blues singers, Rich had talents as deep and varied as rock and roll itself, allowing him to integrate blues, country, pop, and jazz into something that Phillips described to Sun historian Colin Escott as "so effortless . . . I don't think I ever recorded anyone who was better as a singer, writer, and player than Charlie Rich."

Rich arrived at Sun in early 1958 after he and his wife Margaret Ann took a demo of original songs to Bill Justis. He worked at the studio first as a session pianist and songwriter, penning hits for Johnny Cash ("The Ways of a Woman in Love" and "Thanks a Lot"), and writing both sides of Jerry Lee Lewis's 1958 single "Break Up"/"I'll Make It All Up to You," a terrific pairing that sank amid the furor surrounding Lewis's marriage. Rich's first two singles for Phillips International were passable pieces of Presleyesque pop, but the third, "Lonely Weekends," was a full-blown masterpiece, albeit one with plenty of Presley in Rich's vocal. Built around J. M. Van Eaton's snapping drums, Rich's robust piano, and adorned with a corny but somehow perfect vocal chorus, some otherworldly drumshots, and a table-clearing sax break from Martin Willis, "Lonely Weekends" would become both the song that broke Rich nationally and the last great hit produced at Phillips's new digs.

"Lonely Weekends" was Rich's biggest single with Phillips, but many fine sides followed which showcased the breadth of his vast music vocabulary—the slinky blues-pop fusion of "Midnite Blues," the driving rock and roll of "Rebound," the bottomed-out boozer melancholy of "Sittin' and Thinkin'," and the simply astounding "Who Will the Next Fool Be," a bitter, brooding outburst from a scorned, angry lover. (It would become a showstopper for Bobby "Blue" Bland—a man who knew a bit about heartbreak and torment—in 1962.) Many of Rich's best Sun recordings didn't surface until the reissue boom of the eighties, including the swaggering "There Won't Be Anymore," the pounding barrelhouse blues of "Juice Head Blues," and the searing, bitter blues of "Don't Put No Headstone on My Grave," all of which point to the direction—or rather, directions—Rich would go when he left the label in 1963.

He went first to RCA's Groove subsidiary, where he cut some raucous blues swingers to little success. In 1965 he found a home at Smash, where he struck gold almost immediately with the hipster portrait "Mohair Sam" (so slinky even bluesman Slim Harpo had to try his hand at it after Rich took it to the number 21 spot on the *Billboard* pop chart). It was during his two years at Smash that Rich came closest to wedding the myriad influences that surfaced at Sun and Groove—when his blues and country instincts meshed seamlessly with his mastery of pop songcraft. With the exception of "Mohair Sam," though, hits weren't forthcoming, nor did they appear during Rich's 1966–1967 stint with Hi Records, which yielded some of the greatest blue-eyed soul ever recorded—in Memphis, Muscle Shoals, anywhere.

. . . . *J A N E S* . . . .

Charlie was a great talent. Basically they brought him in to be a songwriter, and of course we put down his songs as demos. He had a record that showed a little promise, and then we got into the studio and recorded "Lonely Weekends," which was a combination of the two studios. We recorded the basic record at the old studio, with all the singing and Marty Willis on horn and me and Van Eaton, and then when they opened up the new studio they added the vocal background and a couple other things. The percussion was added here with the new echo chamber. The more you put on it, if it's done right, it comes off good. But then, we didn't want to spend too much money on the records, and if you start getting into violins and voices, that was quite a bit of money back then for a bunch of country boys.

Violins and backing voices would become the hallmarks of Rich's output in the seventies with Epic records, where he and producer Billy Sherrill concocted some of the best and worst records of the countrypolitan era. If you can say that Rich never really sang badly in his life, it's still true that he approached much of the schlock given to him by Sherrill with the workaday perfunctoriness of Elvis slogging through his sixties soundtracks. Painfully shy and ill-equipped to take part in the machinations of star-making, Rich nonetheless found huge success with mediocre ballads such as "Behind Closed Doors" and "The Most Beautiful Girl"—the last hits of his career—but he was clearly walking through them, simply doing his job, far removed from the blues and jazz that fueled his musical passions.

Rich's exasperation imbues what may be his best performance: "Feel Like Going Home," not the string-laden version issued in 1973 on the flipside of "The Most Beautiful Girl" but the one recorded that same year as a demo, on Epic's *Rockabilly Stars, Vol. 1,* with Rich accompanied only by his thoughtful, pained piano playing. In this take the song becomes a stark blues, a contemplation of unshakable failure and fatigue, when the pain becomes crippling. He would turn to it again in 1992, on the gorgeous album *Pictures and Paintings,* (Sire),where he recast it as an almost uplifting spiritual. It was a nice way to end what became the last recordings released before his death in 1995, but it's the '73 demo that defines his genius as it haunts his legacy.

. . . . *J A N E S* . . . .
I think the things Charlie cut later with Billy Sherrill were great records, too. Basically he cut his rock and roll stuff with us and his pop stuff later on, many years later. Charlie had gotten better. There were a lot of people that tried to compare his piano

style to Jerry Lee's. Of course, it was two totally different styles. Charlie was more jazz-oriented and blues, and Jerry Lee was like gospel, country, rock and roll. But they were both great.

You've got to understand: We were evolving. Charlie came on a couple years after I did, and we were evolving. For example, when we got to the "Raunchy" stage, we added horn overdubs to that. It was cut originally with piano, two guitars, and bass and drums, and Bill Justis and his horn. That was almost what you'd call a big-band sound, for what was happening at that time. That was a small room, man. The console had five inputs and you had to make the most with what you had to make it with. I think those records really sound great when you look back on it now and see what was done with what there was to do with it. It blows you away.

🍩

What blows you away more is that Sam Phillips never fully seized the potential so abundant in Charlie Rich's early work. If you're looking for a sign of Phillips's detachment from his label, his studio, and his artists, it's somewhere in his failure to explore the many facets of Rich's talent, the way he did just a few years earlier with Elvis, Johnny Cash, and even second-string country-rockabillies like Warren Smith.

. . . . MOORE . . . .

Sam didn't do a whole bunch after he moved over there. He had myself and a couple other guys that were working there doing sessions. Stan Kesler, Charles Underwood. I think Sam just kind of lost interest in it, personally. He got off into radio stations. That was taking up more of his time, and he more or less turned it over to Bill Justis, Jack Clement, people like that. I don't know if he burned out or what. He still keeps the studio up, but there's not very much going on there. Knox more or less runs the operation, and I don't think he goes there very much. Roland's about the only one there.

I think maybe Sam felt like, well, he did his thing. Plus, he had just started an all-girl radio station and it took a lot of his time getting that rolling. And he was fortunate enough that Kimmons Wilson made him buy some original Holiday Inn stock. He didn't want to do it. He never would say how much he bought, but he said it wasn't much. Kimmons kept after him to get some shares.

Sam and I always got along great, but we parted ways, because while I was going back and forth to Nashville, I cut the album for Epic [1964's *The Guitar That Changed the World*]. He felt like he was let down by that. I had been after him for a couple of years to do some instrumentals and he kept putting it off and putting it off. Epic made me an offer to do that, so I went ahead and did it. Then I moved up to Nashville in '64. I hooked up with them through Billy Sherrill. He had been producing and engineering at the place that Sam bought and he stayed on there for a while, then Epic made him an offer as an A&R man with the Nashville office. We'd become friends through the studio up here and he went to them and wanted to do all Elvis tunes instrumentally. It didn't sell like they thought it would, so that project got dropped after the one record.

*

Having overstayed its welcome by a good five or six years, Sun Records was finally sold on July 1, 1969, to Shelby Singleton, a Nashville music entrepreneur who did promo work in the late fifties for Starday and later served as a producer and A&R man with Mercury, where he cut sides on Brook Benton and Dinah Washington, among others. After establishing his Plantation label in the late sixties, Singleton hit pay dirt with Jeannie C. Riley, who turned Tom T. Hall's "Harper Valley P.T.A." into a chart-topping country-crossover smash.

Although the terms of the deal between Phillips and Singleton were never made public, it is believed that Phillips retained all of his publishing interest and received a percentage of profits yielded by Singleton's new company, dubbed the Sun International Corporation. Under Singleton's reign, Sun became in essence a budget label responsible for dozens of poorly packaged, hastily compiled compendiums of hits by Jerry Lee Lewis, Johnny Cash, Charlie Rich, Roy Orbison, and others. Because Singleton now owned every master recorded for Sun, some of these collections were fattened up with previously unissued recordings, some of which were as good as anything Phillips released in the fifties. (That doesn't excuse Singleton from his involvement with Elvis impersonator Jimmy Ellis, who as the masked "Orion" cut a string of horrible albums for Singleton with telling titles such as *Some Think He Might Be King Elvis*.) It wasn't until Singleton's late-seventies alliance with Charly, an archival label in London, that these outtakes, demos, and rehearsal tapes were presented with the care and appreciation they so obviously deserved.

There is much half-baked, second-rate music among these reissues—rehearsal and alternate takes that carry little in the way of revelation, anthologies of artists who were best served by their previous status as one-single wonders, and boxed sets devoted to the label's tragic demise in the sixties when one carefully selected CD could've told the tale better. Even so, when heard alongside the cream of Sun's output—the stuff that from 1952 to 1959 burst from Sam Phillips's storefront studio and rattled and rebuilt the framework of American culture—the best of these reissues further illuminate the many facets of Phillips's genius and the genius of so many of the men he helped find that place inside themselves where the soul never dies.

. . . . *JANES* . . . .

Sam took all those strange personalities and molded them into something, and he could communicate with them. Even the people that got mad at Sam, almost everybody called him Mr. Phillips. You've got to understand another thing, too, and a lot of people don't realize this: When I cut my first record I was maybe, what, twenty-one? Twenty? And Sam was, what, thirty? Think about that. You know, it's amazing when you stop and think about that. And he'd been doing it before I ever came on the scene. I came on the scene in 1955, and hell, he'd been doing it for four or five years already.

He was an amazing man. I could never really tell you how great I think he is. But all the people were great and there were good people and strange, unique personalities, but once you get that out of the way they were all trying for the same thing. Everybody wanted a hit record and everybody wanted to do the best that they could do. It was a great time, really. I wouldn't trade it for anything.

DISCOGRAPHY

If there's any place in this book to toast the research efforts of Colin Escott and Martin Hawkins, it is here in this discography of the essential Sun albums and compact discs. Thanks to the tireless work of these two British historians—who have been digging through Sam Phillips's tape archive since the late seventies—the story of Sun Records is no longer built around a few hundred 78s and 45s but is a full-blown epic with revised chapters, expanded text, and ample and often fascinating footnotes.

The albums compiled by Escott and Hawkins have been issued by a dizzying number of record companies both in the United States and, even more so, abroad—most notably on the London-based Charly label and Bear Family Records out of West Germany. The collections released over the last ten years by stateside labels such as Rounder, Rhino, and AVI have most often been mere distillations of the more ambitious projects undertaken by the Europeans (who specialize in scale-busting boxed sets loaded with all manner of aural arcana). Whether you're shopping for quantity or quality—and with Sun the two are usually intertwined—it's never been easier to explore the myriad dimensions of the label. Provided, of course, you have a fat bank account and at least a week or two to park yourself in front of the stereo.

Because of the sheer bulk of the label's vast output, not to mention Phillips's fortuitous habit of always letting the tape roll on (thus ensuring the capture of often illuminating outtakes and producer–artist byplay), the Sun legacy is best served by the bodacious boxed sets devoted respectively to its blues, country, and rockabilly eras. Overviews that attempt to pull the three eras together, however, are skimpy affairs that usually hit the obvious highs but seldom touch on some of the more interesting oddities that are also crucial to Sun's history. (It's impossible, for instance, to hear too much of Jerry Lee Lewis's "Whole Lotta Shakin' Goin' On," but Harmonica Frank Floyd's "Rockin' Chair Daddy" demands at least equal time.)

If you insist on buying one such collection, make it *The Sun Records Collection*, a three-CD set on Rhino that's easy to find, relatively inexpensive, and as definitive as a 140-minute skim job can be. If nothing else, it gives you a good idea of just how deep the talent ran at the Memphis studio. It kicks off with Sam Phillips's first-issued blues recording (Joe Hill Louis's ragged-but-right "Gotta Let You Go" from 1950) and ends with the label's last great single (the Jesters's hellacious 1966 rocker "Cadillac Man," featuring the growling vocals of twenty-five-year-old Jim Dickinson). In between you get a sampling of the label's country sides, enough rarities to prime you for a greater taste of Sun ephemera (including the seldom-documented Miller Sisters, one of the few times Phillips proved himself capable of working well with women—in the studio, at least), and the hits that defined the label during its mid-fifties heyday, from Elvis Presley's "That's All Right" and Carl Perkins's

Sam Phillips behind the boards at Sun studio
(Center for Southern Folklore Archives)

"Blue Suede Shoes" to Jerry Lee Lewis's "Whole Lotta Shakin' Goin' On" and Bill Justis's aptly named "Raunchy."

Among the other successful overviews, and the first really great one, is Charly's *The Sun Box*, available now as a two-CD set on Instant but best heard in its original three-album incarnation, which is divided brilliantly into thematic sides specific to blues, rockabilly, country, and the more significant chart hits. Even without Elvis, it's a hell of a raucous, rocking ride, from side one's opening "Rocket 88" (the Jackie Brenston hit from 1951 that may or may not be the first rock and roll record) to the hits finale on side six that concludes with the hard-bopping pop of Charlie Rich's "Lonely Weekends." Charly's *The Sun CD Collection* series presents the label's respective blues, country, and rockabilly singles in chronological order. Again there's no Elvis (RCA has only occasionally licensed the valued Sun masters to outsiders) and no previously unissued material, but the collections are invaluable if you want to take a look at the label's progression and evolution from the viewpoint of a 1950s record-buyer.

Charly's *The Sun Blues Years 1950-1956* isn't just the single greatest collection of Phillips's blues work but arguably the greatest collection of postwar blues, period. This hefty eight-disc assemblage (151 songs in all) spans the gamut of black music in the South—from the crunching electric blues of Howlin' Wolf and Joe Hill Louis to the aching Delta laments of Sleepy John Estes; from the barrelhouse workouts of pianist Mose Vinson to the smooth vocal stylings of the Prisonaires, plus the urban blues of B. B. King, Little Milton, and Billy Emerson. Phillips's rarely heard forays into gospel are present (including the Southern Jubilees's beautiful "Forgive Me Lord"), as are some of Rufus Thomas's seldom-compiled sides (sure, "Bear Cat" is everywhere; his fine take on the Prisonaires' 1953 hit "Walkin' in the Rain" isn't so easy to track down). You also get Willie Nix's relentlessly swinging "Baker Shop Boogie," Big Memphis Ma Rainey's salacious "Baby, No,

No!" Rosco Gordon's "Decorate the Counter" (an anthem of the dead drunk), and Howlin' Wolf's sometime guitarist Pat Hare with the bone-chilling "I'm Gonna Murder My Baby" (which he did in 1960, just six years after recording this prophetic stomper). The lavish booklet (best seen in the full-size edition that came with the since-deleted LP version) includes an extensive interview with Phillips (conducted by Martin Hawkins in 1984) and a session file that also acts as a useful timeline of the label's growth during its earliest stages.

Once you've absorbed *The Sun Blues Years*, move on to Charly's *The Sun Blues Archive* series, a multivolume CD companion to the above-mentioned box featuring a slew of previously unearthed outtakes, alternate versions, and material from vinyl reissues now deleted by the label. Less essential but occasionally revelatory (and a whole lot cheaper) are single-disc domestic collections on Rounder (*Sun Records Harmonica Classics*—the title says it all) and Rhino (*Blue Flames*, a hodgepodge of jump blues, Delta raunch, and gospel).

Howlin' Wolf's complete recordings for Phillips are collected on Bear Family's two-volume *Memphis Days: The Definitive Edition*. Phillips put it best when he said that the Wolf's voice came from a place where the soul of man never dies, but even that statement doesn't prepare you for the emotional exorcisms on both discs. These are some of the most harrowing, abrasive, and throttling recordings in the pantheon of American music—the pathos and terror in the Wolf's gravel-gargling voice on "My Baby Walked Off" and "Moanin' at Midnight," the distortion-laden chords and lead-guitar shrapnel of Willie Johnson on "Baby Ride With Me" and "Mr. Highway Man," the percussive wallop of drummer Willie Steele on "Howlin' Wolf Boogie." Phillips once said that Howlin' Wolf was the greatest artist he ever recorded, greater even than Elvis. Spend a late night with both volumes of *Memphis Days* and you'll probably agree.

Of equal value are the Wolf sides cut in Memphis for the Modern label, collected on Flair's *Howlin' Wolf Rides Again*. There are different versions of songs previously recorded for Phillips, the blazing stompers "Keep What You Got" and "Worried About My Baby," and the simply indescribable "House Rockin' Boogie," a four-minute celebration of self and sound during which the Wolf teaches his band how to dig a deep groove, then jumps into it, admiring its power: "Ain't that sweet?" he asks no one in particular before answering his own question. "Darlin', that's so sweet." Indeed it is.

The best Sun sides by Junior Parker, James Cotton, and Pat Hare are presented on Rounder's *Mystery Train*, where the taut, bare-boned drive of Parker's "Feelin' Good" and "Mystery Train" sets up the shattering "Cotton Crop Blues," a day in the life of harp whiz James Cotton. Two cuts are included by Hare, including "I'm Gonna Murder My Baby." *Delta Rhythm Kings* offers the best look at Ike Turner's early Sun sides, along with related stuff from Raymond Hill, Johnny O'Neal, Billy Emerson, and Ike's first wife, Bonnie Turner (including the must-hear "Way Down in the Congo").

B. B. King's Memphis recordings (for Sun and Modern) can be found on the Ace discs *The Memphis Masters*, *The Best of B. B. King*, and *Do the Boogie*. *The Be-Bop Boy* (Bear Family) at long last rounds up the Sun material of Joe Hill Louis; kindred soul Dr. Isiah Ross (who discovered "The Boogie Disease" in 1954) receives similar treatment on Arhoolie's *His First Recordings*. Little Milton's *The Sun Years* (Rounder) documents an artist in search of a style. Johnny Bragg and the Prisonaires already had one when Phillips arranged for this quintet of jailbirds to be sent from Nashville's Tennessee State Penitentiary to Memphis to cut some of the early fifties' most exquisitely rough-hewn doo-wop. Bear Family's *Just Walkin' in the Rain* collects them all, including the 1953 title hit, one of the greatest Sun ballads not recorded by Elvis or Roy Orbison. Rosco Gordon's recordings for Phillips—leased in the early fifties to the Chess, RPM, and Duke labels—are best heard on Charly's *Rosco's Rhythm*. That rhythm could come on big and boozy, sweet and slinky, and occasionally with a Caribbean slink-and-shimmy that faintly recalled the second-line boogie of piano ace Professor Longhair.

Mississippi bluesman Frank Frost has the distinction of being the last artist to cut a blues session with Phillips. The fruits of that 1962 session were issued on the unjustly overlooked Phillips International album *Hey, Boss Man!* reissued on CD by Charly. To hear it is to become even more frustrated at Phillips's growing detachment from his label and studio, not to mention his mid-fifties abandonment of the blues following the arrival of Elvis. As for Rufus Thomas—perceived by many as a marginally gifted novelty artist although cherished rightly by Memphians as the living embodiment of black-music history—there isn't one collection devoted solely to his pre-Stax recordings. In all there were fourteen sides issued: Five show up on *The Sun Blues Years* (Charly); four others are available on the excellent if occasionally scattershot Euro-bootleg series *Stompin'* ("The Easy Livin' Plan" on Volume Three, "Decorate the Counter" on Volume Eleven, and "No More Doggin' Around" and "Crazy About You Baby" on Volume Nineteen). Rhino's *Do the Funky Somethin': The Best of Rufus Thomas* includes only "Bear Cat" amid the usual assortment of Stax hits such as "Walking the Dog" and "Do the Funky Chicken." It's a good set to be sure, but it could've easily been better.

Depending on who you ask, you'll hear that Sam Phillips either didn't have much of an ear for country-and-western or he simply didn't care much about competing with the big boys in Nashville. Certainly *The Sun Country Years*, an overwhelmingly exhaustive eleven-album box on Bear Family, supports both statements. But amid the numbing and innumerable mediocrities lurks a formidable body of recordings that support the romantic notion of Memphis as an outpost of honky-tonk oddballs.

Wade through the boxed set if you must (and I don't blame you, since it's one of the few places you can turn up a good chunk of stuff by Harmonica Frank Floyd), but I prefer the more coherent and consistent single-disc collections on AVI: *Defrost Your Heart* and *Drink Up and Go Home*, where the eccentricities of Charlie Feathers hang tight with the beer-stained melancholy of Carl Perkins's early sides (cut when he was still shaking the ghost of Hank Williams), and where the one-shot keepers of Ernie Chaffin ("I'm Lonesome"), the Dixieland Drifters ("I'm Gonna Find Her"), and Slim Rhodes ("Romp and Stomp") meld masterfully with lesser-known nuggets from Johnny Cash and Jerry Lee Lewis. Rhino's *Memphis Ramble* offers a brief (eighteen cuts) but excellent overview of the treasures available on the Bear Family box, among them Bill Taylor and Smokey Joe's "Split Personality" (a masterful novelty record worthy of Hasil Adkins), Malcolm Yelvington's strutting "It's Me Baby," and Charlie Feathers's aching, forlorn "Man in Love" (the best of his country sides before he began mastering rockabilly; see other albums detailed below).

So unclassifiable is the artistry of Harmonica Frank Floyd that his sides cut with Phillips would fit perfectly on any Sun blues, country, or rockabilly compilation. They crop up usually in the company of Sun's straight-country artists, but the best place to discover them is on Puritan's impossible-to-locate but ostensibly in print *The Great Original Recordings*, still awaiting a CD release. For a glimpse at honky-tonk straddling the fence post of rockabilly, check out Malcolm Yelvington's *Gonna Have Myself a Ball: The Complete 1950s Recordings* (Charly), which offers an entertaining look at one of the more interesting footnotes in Sun's pre-Elvis history.

Some of Charlie Feathers's best early recordings—including fine alternate takes of "Defrost Your Heart"—can be found on Zu-Zazz's *Rock-A-Billy*. Good as he was as a country balladeer, Feathers was always most convincing as a rockabilly (after all, he invented it, or so he claims). He mastered the form not at

Sun, however, but at King Records in Cincinnati with mid-fifties' piledrivers such as "One Hand Loose," "Bottle to the Baby," and "Nobody's Woman" (available along with his 1956 Meteor single "Tongue-Tied Jill" and other stray items on Charly's *Gone Gone Gone* CD and Kay's *Jungle Fever* LP). *Tip Top Daddy* (Norton) brings together twenty-four acoustic demos from the late fifties to the early seventies. *Uh Huh Honey*, another Norton disc, exhumes some fine sixties and seventies sides, including the late sixties tracks issued on Barrelhouse's discontinued *That Rockabilly Cat!* LP. Feathers's passion and commitment to rockabilly also come through on the 1991 disc *Charlie Feathers* (Elektra/Nonesuch), a marginally successful collection produced by Ben Vaughn and featuring Sun vets Roland Janes, Stan Kesler, and J. M. Van Eaton. Certainly there is a need for a compilation drawn from all parts of Feathers's vast and often fascinating career. Until that need is filled, you have to amass a huge pile of Feathers product to discern the origin of his considerable cult following.

As for Feathers's nemesis, Elvis Presley, every known side cut by him at Sun—the issued masters and all known alternate takes—is available on RCA's *The Complete Sun Sessions*. (Of course there are probably a few outtakes lying in wait in the back of RCA's tape vaults, but who knows for sure? And who knows exactly when they'll be retrieved?) If you're willing to do without a few negligible alternate takes, opt for the five-CD *Elvis: The King of Rock 'n' Roll—The Complete 50's Masters*, which presents the Sun material in the best fidelity yet alongside the RCA material that immediately followed.

I'm not sure what there is left to say about Elvis's Sun records. So much has already been written by men and women who have defined with authority the appeal and importance of these recordings—the context in which they were created, the foundations they crumbled and rebuilt, the place they occupy in America's history and popular culture. Myself, these records leave me something that's pretty close to speechless; I don't know that I'll ever be able to pinpoint exactly the effect they have on me. I will say that I can't go more than three or four months before something compels me to pull them off the CD shelf. Sometimes the occasion is the anniversary of his August 16 death or his January 8 birthday, or catching one of the coinciding TV reruns of the amazing *Elvis '56* documentary. Maybe some smartass at work will make a Fat Elvis joke and I'll feel the need to compensate for the blasphemy. Or maybe I'll grow infuriated after listening to a recently purchased bootleg of what turns out to be the usual hodgepodge of fourth- and fifth-rate rockabilly frauds and I'll need to remind myself just how good the music really is.

And every time I do I stand back and marvel at the agility and grace and determination with which Elvis, Scotty Moore, and Bill Black approached Roy Brown's "Good Rockin' Tonight" and Arthur Crudup's "That's All Right," at the way they turned Arthur Gunter's perfectly mediocre "Baby, Let's Play House" into a thundering culmination of everything they'd pulled off following that first night at Sun. I wonder if I'll ever stop getting chills when "Blue Moon" pours from the speakers, or if I'll ever not laugh out loud when Elvis does just that as "Mystery Train" winds to a close. (Likewise, will I ever stop wondering how he could laugh at all after tearing so ferociously into what is the most unnerving and gripping of his Sun sides?) Beyond those questions, and dozens of others just like them, I only know one thing for sure: Nothing that's ever been written about Elvis Presley and the Sun recordings comes anywhere near defining for you just how good this music is. You just have to hear them.

The argument in defense of Presley's seriously underrated sixties and seventies work is too lengthy to get into here, and it seems insane to even think of having to defend songs as great as "Can't Help Falling in Love," "Spinout," "You Don't Know Me," "Long Black Limousine," "Suspicious Minds," and "I Can Help." But there remain a lot of myths and heresy surrounding

the final two-thirds of the Presley oeuvre, so for the misin-
formed souls who think that *The Complete 50's Masters* is all the
Elvis they'll ever need I offer a brief shopping list, in roughly
chronological order and all issued on RCA: *From Nashville to
Memphis: The Essential 60's Masters I; Command Performances:
The Essential 60's Masters II; Spinout; February, 1970: On Stage;
That's the Way It Is; Elvis Country; Elvis Now; Elvis (a.k.a. Fool);
Good Times; Promised Land; Elvis Today; Walk a Mile in My Shoes:
The Essential 70's Masters;* and *Moody Blue.*

To get an idea of how drastically Elvis improved on his R&B
and blues sources, see *Elvis Classics* (P-Vine, Japan) a pricey but
interesting assortment of tunes covered—or is that bettered?—
by Elvis. Even better, but unfortunately as-yet-unreleased, is an
undertaking of Andy Franklin's mentioned by Peter Guralnick
in the discography of his Elvis bio *Last Train to Memphis: The
Rise of Elvis Presley:* namely, a collection of the first thirty songs
covered by Elvis to be titled *Fit for a King*—a licensing night-
mare to be sure, but a damn fine idea just the same.

So great is Jerry Lee Lewis's artistry that any collection of his
Sun recordings—even those horrid albums slapped together in
the seventies by Shelby Singleton—will supply ample proof of
his genius. It's *Classic—Jerry Lee Lewis* (Bear Family), however,
that defines just how expansive and encompassing that genius
actually is. The eight CDs present the Killer's complete Sun
recordings—246 songs in all, remastered in brilliant, shimmer-
ing mono (save 56 stereo cuts from the later years). Moving
from creaky old standards to Southern gospel, from rock and
roll readymades to prewar blues and gospel, Jerry Lee tackles
the twentieth-century American songbook like it was written
for him. After hearing him blaze through "The Marine Band
Hymn" like a one-man battalion, you'll believe it was. To call
this the finest Jerry Lee Lewis set ever assembled doesn't do
the man nor the set any kind of justice; call it simply the finest
boxed set on the planet. If you must settle for something small-

er, try on Bear Family's single disc *Up Through the Years* and Rhino's *Rare Tracks*. But trust me, you need the box.

Lewis left Sun in 1963 to sign with Nashville's Mercury Records. If his career at that point was already a shambles (and it was), his initial recordings for Mercury didn't bode well for the future, unless you thought the best way to reintroduce the Killer to the record-buying public was through remakes of his Sun hits (and it wasn't). Then, at the insistence of Mercury producer Eddie Kilroy, the label had Lewis do some straight country numbers. And something happened: Suddenly all the pain, anger, and disillusionment that had dogged Lewis through the hitless years following the marriage scandal was poured into the music—songs about cheating and songs of being cheated on, gospel relics and hoary Tin Pan Alley standards, honky-tonk classics and written-to-orders that soon would become classic. There were covers of current hits that often obliterated the originals and new songs that mirrored his soul so perfectly that they seemed to be dictated by Lewis to the toilers of the Music City's songmill.

The result was a fabulous string of hits and a body of work that very nearly rivals the axis-tilters gathered on the Sun box. They're available in myriad reissues: Bear Family's *The Locust Years* (eight CDs) and the three-volume *The Killer* (each featuring between nine and eleven albums); and, most cogently, *Killer: The Mercury Years* (three CDs on Mercury). There are several single-disc overviews which merely present the hits—among them "Another Place, Another Time," "One Has My Heart," and "What's Made Milwaukee Famous (Has Made a Loser Out of Me)"—but as with Lewis's Sun years, you need to hear everything to fully gauge the staggering breadth and depth of this man's talent. (And while you're at it, look for Rhino's *Live at the Star-Club Hamburg*, an incendiary set from 1964 that ranks high alongside such concert classics as James Brown's *Live at the Apollo, 1962* and Otis Redding's *Live in Europe*.)

The glorious rise and tragic fall of Carl Perkins—who as much as Elvis helped create and perfect the fine art of rockabilly—is presented on *The Classic Carl Perkins*. Yet another boxed set on Bear Family, *Classic* includes everything Perkins cut during his three years at Sun—including a few alternate takes that outshine their issued counterparts—as well as the Columbia and Decca sides he cut once he flew the Phillips coop in 1957. You can find more succinct and consistently entertaining Perkins collections (try Bear Family's *Up Through the Years*), but it's only on *Classic* where you can hear the man's singular brand of rockabilly develop, flourish, and (sadly) dissipate.

Although some critics have made the mistake of confusing Perkins with the true visionaries of rock and roll, *Classic* establishes the man as exactly what he was—rockabilly's most wildly gifted artist, a combination vocalist-lyricist-guitarist-bandleader with no peers in the genre. (You could make an argument for Gene Vincent, I guess, but I've heard his Capitol box and I'm not buying it—the box or the argument.) For a few brief years in the mid-fifties, Perkins defined rockabilly like no one this side of Elvis. He was as weird as rockabilly's weirdest (e.g., "Her Love Rubbed Off") and he sang with the force of a jump-blues shouter, but the twang in his voice was as country as a jug of Tennessee corn liquor. And his guitar had twice the kick, slashing like a straight razor through burlap on even a contrived pop throwaway like "Your True Love" and popping like a string of firecrackers on "Everybody's Trying to Be My Baby."

"Blue Suede Shoes" is Perkins's sole hit and acclaimed masterpiece, but I've always leaned more to "Dixie Fried," a roadhouse vignette full of wicked humor and drunken violence. Too bad he couldn't sustain that kind of writing through the sixties, instead of having the Beatles carry on his legacy with their comparatively tepid Perkins covers. Although his late-sixties sides with Columbia and Decca contained a few treasures, everything that's followed has been mediocre at best, embarrassing at worst.

Johnny Cash has never had much trouble sustaining a career, and he's done it for the better part of forty years without changing that much. Arriving at Sun in 1955 with an unusual voice and a band to match, Cash and the bass-guitar combo of Marshall Grant and Luther Perkins struck immediate pay dirt with their first single—a pairing of the Cash-penned "Cry, Cry, Cry" and "Hey Porter." In a studio where strange sounds were as common as humidity during a Memphis summer, the Cash trio were genuine oddballs. The rudimentary bass thumps from Grant, Perkins's primitive lead breaks, the rhythmic click-clack of Cash's acoustic guitar (achieved by weaving a piece of paper in and out of the strings), and Cash's dark, booming baritone, which sometimes went as flat as a day-old beer—they weren't exactly the kind of combo you'd expect to yield more country and pop hits than any other Sun act. But that's what they did throughout Cash's three-year stint at the label, cranking out numerous classics along the way, including "Folsom Prison Blues," "Big River," "Train of Love," "Home of the Blues," and "Get Rhythm."

Much as I love the Cash sound at Sun, I've always found the behemoth boxed sets on Charly and Bear Family—*The Sun Years* and *Classic Johnny Cash, 1954–1958* (which also includes his first Columbia recordings)—to be too much of a good thing. Have at 'em if you wish, but I'll stick with Bear Family's generous and definitive single-disc set *Up Through the Years.* To hear the cream of his Sun work within the context of his occasionally inspired recordings with Columbia (the label he joined after leaving Sun), look for Columbia/Legacy's three-disc *The Essential Johnny Cash 1955-83.* (Avoid Charly's half-assed *Country Boy,* a twenty-five-cut CD that baffling omits the great hit "Home of the Blues." If you can't locate *Up Through the Years,* Rhino's *The Sun Years* will suffice.) *Johnny Cash at Folsom Prison* (now available in tandem with the lesser *Johnny Cash at San Quentin*) is a sometimes frightening, loose-limbed set of gallows humor and boogie that may be country music's greatest live album.

After coasting through most of the seventies and eighties, struggling with his various addictions and making mostly lousy albums, Cash rebounded in 1994 with *American Recordings*, produced by one-time hip-hop avatar Rick Rubin and issued on his American label. Featuring just Cash's acoustic guitar and his effectively craggy voice, *American Recordings* was remarkable for the commitment and conviction the man brought to the music; it was the first time he sounded interested in his material since he returned to the old stuff on the 1988 *Classic Cash/Hall of Fame Series* (Polygram) and its sterling follow-up *Water from the Wells of Home* (Polygram, 1988). If on *American Recordings* he managed to make his own the songs of Leonard Cohen, Tom Waits, Glenn Danzig, and Loudon Wainwright III, the formula-repeating *Unchained* (American, 1996, with ace liner notes from Cash) found him floundering with ill-suited material. Of course, no one could redeem the awful likes of Beck's "Rowboat."

Even if a single note hadn't been caught on tape, just the story behind the music on RCA's *The Million Dollar Quartet* would ensure its place in the pantheon of great rock and roll tales. It's been told a thousand times, so I'll be brief: On December 4, 1956, Elvis Presley paid a visit to his old buddies at Sun. Carl Perkins was there cutting a session with Jerry Lee Lewis on piano and Jack Clement running the board. Knowing a great photo op when he saw one, Phillips got on the horn to *Commercial Appeal* reporter Robert Johnson, who hurried to the studio in time to get a shot of Presley, Perkins, Lewis, and Johnny Cash (who got a call from Phillips to come down to the studio for the photo). Johnson dubbed the bunch the Million Dollar Quartet.

What ensued was a loose, informal gospel jam not unlike the sessions Presley used to warm up before studio dates. From the piano he led the trio through gospel standards and country hits, rock and roll songs from Chuck Berry, and a fascinating segment in which Elvis talks about hearing a young R&B singer in Las Vegas—actually Jackie Wilson during his stint with the Dominos—singing the hell out of his "Don't Be Cruel." ("Man, he cut me," Elvis admits. "I was under the table when he got through singin'.") You also hear a very young Jerry Lee playing the songs from his just-released debut single "End of the Road," clearly trying to drag Elvis into something like a cutting match. (Elvis, ever the gentleman, demurs.)

Just as *The Million Dollar Quartet* isn't so much an album as a document, the songs on the disc are more like fragments, snippets of faintly remembered lyrics, a melody hummed with more passion than precision, and a lighthearted ambience that overrides the poor fidelity of the session. Nevertheless, as documents go, *The Million Dollar Quartet* is invaluable, a moment of historic preservation tantamount to discovering a recording of Babe Ruth saying that, hell yes he called that shot at Wrigley Field.

Great as the real story is, I've always harbored a fantasy about the Million Dollar Quartet in which Billy Lee Riley appeared to make it a fivesome. Already an established studio player at Sun with a few intense rockers issued on the label (some of which featured Jerry Lee on piano), Riley was maybe the only Sun artist there who could've gone after Elvis with more gusto, relish, and determination than the Killer. At least that's the impression you get after hearing the manic rockers that have made Riley a deserving icon among rockabilly cultists, who love hardcore rockers with no chart hits to sully their glorious obscurity.

Where do you assign blame for Riley's poor faring in the fifties? I say throw half of it at Phillips and the rest at Riley himself. Because there wasn't any love lost between Sam and Billy Lee, Phillips never nurtured Riley's talent the way he did with Elvis or Carl Perkins. And Riley needed nurturing: Unable to harness his deep love of honky-tonk and blues and turn them into something really different (the way Jerry Lee did, for instance), Riley moved wantonly from blazing rockers and plaintive country-and-western to interpretations of his favorite blues hits. Of course, Riley's lack of direction or focus doesn't diminish the raw power and unbridled enthusiasm of "Red Hot," "Flying Saucer Rock and Roll," "No Name Girl," and the other Riley winners collected by Bear Family on the double-disc *The Classic Recordings* and AVI on the *Red Hot: The Best of Billy Lee Riley* CD.

Little remains of the countless singles and albums Riley recorded after his stint at Sun (even "Kay," his definitive reading of the John Wesley Ryles tune recorded in 1969 for Shelby Singleton's Sun International, is out of print). To be sure, there were many lousy sides for many major and indie labels. A collection that highlighted the best of them—including the wickedly rocking instrumental "Shimmy Shimmy Walk," his white-soul take on Tony Joe White's "I've Got a Thing About You Baby"—would serve Riley's legacy well. Until it arrives, you can make do with *Blue Collar Blues* (HighTone, 1994), a great set of white blues and revived rockabilly recorded at Phillips's studio with former Little Green Men Roland Janes and J. M. Van Eaton, among others.

Like Riley, neither Roy Orbison nor Charlie Rich reached his full potential at Sun. Orbison arrived at the studio in 1956 from the map-speck Texas town of Wink, a honky-tonker inspired by Elvis with one single already to his credit ("Ooby Dooby" backed with a tentative version of the Eagles' R&B hit "Trying to Get to You," bettered at Sun by Elvis in 1955). Rich, meanwhile, was an Arkansas pianist whose musicianship and taste for jazz caught the ear of Sun music director, saxophonist, and resident rock-hater Bill Justis. (When Rich first showed up at the studio to play his demo tape for Justis, he was handed a stack of Sun singles and told to listen to them and come back when he was that bad.) Though both men had to leave Sun in order to make the music they felt inside—Orbison went to

Monument, Rich to a series of labels, most notably Smash, Hi, and Epic—each left his mark at 706.

The Orbison sessions overseen by Sun engineer Jack Clement were marked by the singer's high, nervous tenor, which added to the emotional turbulence in the pained ballad "Devil Doll" as well as the galloping rocker "Problem Child" (in which poor Roy has to contend with a bop-addled girlfriend—"Don't you see this shaking spree is going to be the death of me?"). Even the masterful hipster portrait "Domino," driven by two wicked solos by guitarist James Morrow, is underpinned by the resigned envy in Orbison's vocal (which is in stark contrast to Dr. Horse's thematically linked fifties oddity "Jack, That Cat Was Clean," an R&B homage to a sharp-dressed ladykiller). Maybe "Domino" was actually a wishful alter ego for Orbison, who was never what you'd call a matinee idol. Whatever the case, the above-mentioned songs, along with the priceless "Rockhouse," "Go Go Go," and the demo for "Claudette" (a hit for the Everly Brothers in 1958), are gathered on Bear Family's definitive *The Sun Years 1956–58*.

For Orbison's majestic and haunted (or is that haunting?) Monument hits, consult *All-Time Greatest Hits of Roy Orbison* (Monument) or *The Legendary* boxed set on Sony, which spans the gamut of Orbison's career. After spending most of the seventies and eighties on the oldies touring circuit, Orbison's career was revitalized in 1986 after the startlingly effective use of his 1963 hit "In Dreams" in David Lynch's creepy film *Blue Velvet*. The comeback trail led him in 1988 to the Traveling Wilburys, a supergroup of sorts that also included Bob Dylan, George Harrison, Tom Petty, and Jeff Lynne (see *The Traveling Wilburys Volume One* [Warner Bros.] for Orbison's breathtakingly beautiful "Not Alone Any More"). Next up was *Mystery Girl,* a muddled but commercially successful affair issued just weeks before his 1988 death and featuring an all-star line-up (Jeff Lynne, Elvis Costello, Bono, and the Edge, et al) doing their best to overwhelm the delicacy and grace of Orbison's artistry. To hear and see what Orbison could do within a star-studded setting, rent a copy of HBO Video's 1988 release *A Black and White Night*, during which Orbison and a cast of Bruce Springsteen, guitar slinger James Burton, and others turn in masterful versions of "Only the Lonely," "(All I Can Do Is) Dream You," and especially "Dream Baby." The camaraderie of the ensemble cuts through the somewhat pretentious cinematography, and though Springsteen took a few critical shots for what was perceived as a mugging performance, it looks to me like he's just having one hell of a good time. Which he no doubt was.

Although it's infuriatingly incomplete, the 1997 double-disc *Feel Like Going Home: The Essential Charlie Rich* is the only place where you can hear in one place his evolution, his assimilation of Southern R&B, urbane jazz, fifties pop, and the kind of rock and roll ushered in by Elvis and Sam Phillips. And that's more a tribute to Rich's greatness, since the set overlooks many of the man's best sides. Only four Sun tunes are presented; his groundbreaking and soulful work with Groove and Hi are represented by a measly three cuts from the former, one from the latter. You get only six samples of his apex years at Smash, and many of his finest Epic recordings with Billy Sherrill are side-stepped entirely.

If you're only looking for a quick Rich fix, *Feel Like Going Home* will do. All others are advised to seek out the following: *Lonely Weekends: The Best of the Sun Years* (AVI); *Don't Put No Headstone On My Grave* (Zu-Zazz, featuring the complete session that produced the title cut and remixed versions of a few hits and misses in which the strings and backing choruses have been removed—fine for something like "My Heart Cries Out for You," but "Lonely Weekends" without those bizarre backing chants is like "Louie Louie" with a remixed vocal); *Charlie Rich* (an out-of-print album on Groove); *The Complete Smash Sessions* (Mercury); *Charlie Rich Sings the Songs of Hank Williams Plus the R&B Sessions* (Diablo/Demon, twenty-five songs culled from his 1966–1967 sessions at Hi Records in Memphis); *Set Me Free* and *The Fabulous Charlie Rich* (vintage Epic albums reissued on Koch/Sony); *Silver Linings* (a deleted Epic set from 1976); and *Pictures and Paintings* (his triumphant 1992 return on Sire Records). Rich died in 1995.

That pretty much covers the kingpins of Sun—that is, the artists who set the tone and laid the groundwork for the others that followed, few of whom were able to produce more than a few worthwhile cuts. The problem had something to do with roots: Where Elvis Presley, Jerry Lee Lewis, Carl Perkins, and Billy Lee Riley summoned their music from the deep traditions of Southern blues, gospel, and country-and-western, many of the rest simply aped the innovations of the Phillips bunch. When they tore into a blues cover, their model was Elvis, and it showed. (And none of these men, even the most demented rockers in the bunch, had a thing on Elvis.) That's not to make an argument for any elitist notion of musical purity or divine inheritance of the right influences; think of it as the difference between the gifted R.E.M. deriving inspiration from the Byrds and the Velvet Underground, and the not-so-gifted Connells and the Windbreakers drawing theirs from R.E.M.

Arguably the greatest also-ran at Sun was Warren Smith. He actually threatened to break into the mainstream with the Johnny Cash-penned "Rock 'n' Roll Ruby" and the Roy Orbison readymade "So Long, I'm Gone" (which cracked the *Billboard* Hot 100 when it was released in 1957). And though future hits weren't forthcoming, the evidence at hand on *The Classic Recordings* (Bear Family) also proves Smith was a fine country singer with a robust voice and a blues-kissed sense of phrasing. Although unissued at the time, Smith's 1957 "Red Cadillac and a Black Mustache" is one of the greatest things ever recorded at Sun and is maybe the record that would've broken him nationally. Instead he had to wait until the early sixties, when he hooked up with Liberty Records in Nashville for a few moderately successful singles.

After Smith, the quality at Sun dropped slightly, with an endless line of wannabe rockers retooling their honky-tonk bop in an effort to prick Phillips's ear. Sonny Burgess knocked out a few raving rockers and wailing blues covers, worth hearing mostly for his growling vocals and slashing guitar work. Even the best of them—"Red Headed Woman," "We Wanna Boogie," "Ain't Gonna Do It," collected on Bear Family's double-disc *The Classic Sun Recordings* and AVI's more manageable *Hittin' That Jug! The Best of Sonny Burgess* CD—get by more on the energy of Burgess and his group the Pacers than anything you'd ever confuse with greatness. Similarly, his most recent albums (1992's Dave Alvin-produced *Tennessee Border* on HighTone and *Sonny Burgess*, released by Rounder in 1996) are full of good ideas that never quite click. Nor do most of the items retrieved from the 1959 session of Michigan rockabilly Johnny Powers on Norton's *Long Blond Hair*, which also rounds up his pre-Sun singles on *Fox and Fortune*. It's worth checking out, though, for the drooling "Be Mine, All Mine." Everything you'll ever need by Bill Justis is on the 1969 Sun International collection *Raunchy*, ostensibly out of print but easy to find in the used bins. He may have hated rock and roll, but he was pretty damn good at it (e.g., "Raunchy," "College Man").

Astounding as it may seem, there isn't one definitive collection of Sun's vast rockabilly recordings—meaning one that digs as deeply into this seemingly bottomless well as Bear Family's country-themed boxed set without overlooking the label's first-string sluggers. Of course, that doesn't mean the obscurities haven't been compiled to death, most notably on Charly's staggering twelve-album box *Sun Records—The Rockin' Years*, a great place to scoop up a mess of rare rockers but a wildly inconsistent set nonetheless.

More manageable was *The Roots of Rock*, Charly's sadly deleted line of LP reissues from the late seventies which included several fascinating volumes. My favorites of the bunch are the pair of *Rebel Rockabilly* comps and *The Best of Sun Rockabilly*

Volumes One and Two. (Before you go plundering the used-vinyl bins, be forewarned: Charly's LP reissues from this period were marred by shoddy remastering; their CDs issued in the late eighties are slightly better.) If you want only the obvious rockers, try RCA's seventeen-track *Sun's Greatest Hits*, not the most imaginatively compiled disc but the first Sun collection to include anything by Elvis. AVI's expertly remastered trio of Sun rockabilly volumes—*Let's Bop, Rock Baby, Rock It*, and *Rock Boppin' Baby*—rounds up seventy-two mostly magnificent obscurities from great one-shot boppers such as Jack Earls, Tommy Blake, Hayden Thompson, and Ray Harris (whose explosive "Come On Little Mama" predated the punkabilly fusion of the Cramps and Memphis's Panther Burns by a good twenty years). Rounder's *Sun Rockabilly: The Classic Recordings* doesn't quite live up to its title, but it's easy to find and includes essentials by Billy Lee Riley ("Red Hot," "Flying Saucer Rock and Roll"), Hayden Thompson (covering Little Junior Parker's "Love My Baby," the flip to his 1953 Sun hit "Mystery Train"), and Edwin Bruce's leering "Rock Boppin' Baby."

With a few notable exceptions, *The Rockin' 60s* (Charly) is the most depressing item in the Sun reissue canon, a boxed-set reminder of just how far the label slid in the sixties—lazy rock, lame country, and smarmy pop. The exception on *The Rockin' 60s* is the throttling stuff cut during two 1966 sessions by Jim Dickinson's Jesters. Only two cuts were issued at the time— "Cadillac Man" and its flipside "My Babe"—and Dickinson says a few other tracks have disappeared. But for a couple of nights in Memphis, the Jesters attacked the material with a kind of manic purpose, like they knew it was up to them not only to redeem all the garbage that had been flooding out of Phillips's new studio, but to remind anyone who listened that when Sun Records rocked, they were untouchable.

Hearing him howl like a rabid dog on "Cadillac Man," one shudders at the thought of what Dickinson might have done if he'd been about ten years younger and showed up at Sun just before or after Billy Lee Riley and Jerry Lee Lewis. As it is you'll have to make do with the two surviving pieces of Dickinson's pre-Jesters history: "Monkey Man" and "Shake 'em On Down," howling and intense white blues from a 1965 single issued by Dickinson's Katmandu Quartet on the Southtown label (a subsidiary of Monument). Available at this writing only on the British various-artists set *Shakin' Black* (Still), the Katmandu single is both a harbinger of the Jesters' insanity to come and the course Dickinson's long, eclectic career would take. (Sadly, no one has yet compiled "You'll Do It All the Time," Dickinson's 1964 recording debut with the Beale Street Sheiks.)

Since most of Dickinson's reputation is based on his skills as a session pianist and producer, there are pitiful few examples of his greatness as a bandleader and a vocalist. (Well, really he's a screamer, but he's a mighty screamer.) His one proper solo album, 1972's *Dixie Fried* (Atlantic) has bewilderingly eluded both bootleggers and the preservationist hotshots at Rhino (who flooded the racks in the early nineties with all kinds of Atlantic reissues). Two essential Dickinson vocals—on "Red Hot" and a scorching version of Lightnin' Slim's "Rooster Blues"—liven up the otherwise lackluster Johnny Burnette's *Rock and Roll Trio and Their Rockin' Friends from Memphis*, a tribute album issued in 1980 on Rock-A-Billy Records and featuring the likes of Trio guitarist Paul Burlison, Charlie Feathers (sounding all kinds of tore up on "Gone and Left Me Blues"), Eddie Bond, and many other Memphis rockabilly survivors.

Dickinson's mid-eighties recordings as one-fourth of the mangy blues group Mud Boy and the Neutrons are assembled on *They Walk Among Us* (Koch International). *Delta Experimental Projects Compilation Volume 2: Spring Poems* (Fan Club, 1990) is a collection of Dickinson's spoken verse and ambient sound textures. Interesting to say the least, but nothing there rivals "Cut

Me at 7½," a beat-flavored journal recitation written during an early-seventies European tour with Ry Cooder and recorded in 1992 with his sons Luther and Cody Dickinson. (See *Hambone's Meditations,* a various-artists EP issued on the Memphis-based Sugar Ditch label.) To get an idea of Dickinson's virtuosity behind the production board over the years, consult the following: Ry Cooder's *Boomer's Story* (Reprise); Big Star's *Third/Sister Lovers* (Rykodisc CD); Alex Chilton's *Like Flies on Sherbert* (Peabody LP); the Replacements' *Pleased to Meet Me* (Reprise); and Toots Hibbert's *Toots in Memphis* (Mango).

As Jim Dickinson will tell you, any story of Sun Records or Memphis music in general is in essence the story of Dewey Phillips, the legendary disc jockey who in the 1950s used his WHBQ show "Red Hot and Blue" to expose the Mid-South masses to the power, beauty, and importance of the blues—and later, rock and roll. Phillips wasn't the only white DJ in America spinning blues and R&B sides in the early fifties, but his taste was impeccable (Sister Rosetta Tharpe's "Strange Things Happening Every Day" was among his favorites) and his crazed spiels and manic patter may help explain why so many crazed and manic records were produced in Memphis back in the fifties. He was the first DJ in America to play Elvis's first single, but beyond that he was the embodiment of radio's possibilities during both the golden age of R&B and the dawn of rock and roll, as much a personality—an entity—for his listeners as any of the artists lucky enough to get their records slapped on the Phillips turntable.

About an hour's worth of Dewey Phillips transcripts spanning the years 1952–1964 are available on *Red Hot and Blue* (Memphis Archives CD), a wild, hilarious rollercoaster ride through a funhouse of motormouthed dementia, first-rate R&B, and about a thousand plugs for C.V. Beer ("You know, it just ain't no baseball game unless you got a good ol' cold bottle of C.V. in your hand, or maybe a case on the left side!"). Marvel at Phillips's brilliant madness and laugh yourself drunk from the garbled, frantic, but always on-the-money sales pitches. But prepare to sober up when you start thinking about who may have been listening to these very broadcasts as they were shot alive and kicking through the Memphis airwaves. As much as anything ever issued on the golden-yellow Sun label, this, too, is a part of the story.

BIBLIOGRAPHY

Booth, Stanley. *Rhythm Oil: A Journey Through the Music of the American South*. Pantheon, 1991.

Cohn, Lawrence, ed. *Nothing But the Blues*. Abbeville Press, 1993.

Davis, Hank. "Rosco Gordon." *Living Blues*. Winter 1980–81.

Escott, Colin, with Hawkins, Martin. *Good Rockin' Tonight: Sun Records and the Birth of Rock 'n' Roll*. St. Martin's Press, 1991.

Escott, Colin. *Classic Jerry Lee Lewis*. Bear Family Records. 1989.

Graves, Tom. Unpublished interview with Rufus Thomas. May 2, 1994.

Guralnick, Peter. *Lost Highway: Journeys and Arrivals of American Musicians*. David R. Godine, 1979.

Guralnick, Peter. *Sweet Soul Music: Rhythm and Blues and the Southern Dream of Freedom*. Harper & Row, 1986.

Guralnick, Peter. *Last Train to Memphis: The Rise of Elvis Presley*. Little, Brown, 1994.

Hawkins, Martin. *Sun Records: The Blues Years, 1950–1956*. Charly Records, 1985.

Kelly, Michael. "Lasting Legacy." *The Commercial Appeal* (Memphis), June 30, 1996.

Kingsbury, Paul, ed. *Country: The Music and the Musicians*. Abbeville Press, 1988.

Marcus, Greil. *Mystery Train: Images of America in Rock 'n' Roll Music*. E. P. Dutton, 1975.

Marsh, Dave. *Elvis*. Times Books, 1982.

Marsh, Dave. *The Heart of Rock & Soul: The 1,001 Greatest Singles Ever Made*. Plume, 1989.

Morrison, Craig. *Go Cat Go: Rockabilly Music and Its Makers*. University of Illinois Press, 1996.

Palmer, Robert. *Jerry Lee Lewis Rocks!* Delilah, 1981.

Palmer, Robert. *Deep Blues*. Viking Press, 1981.

Shaw, Arnold. *Honkers and Shouters: The Golden Years of Rhythm and Blues*. Macmillan, 1978.

Toshes, Nick. *Country: The Biggest Music in America.* Dell, 1997.

Whitburn, Joel. *Top R&B Singles 1942–1995.* Record Research, 1996.

Whitburn, Joel. *Top Pop Singles 1955–1993.* Record Research, 1987.

Whitburn, Joel. *Top Country Singles 1944–1993.* Record Research, 1994.

INDEX

A

Ace, Johnny, 3, 9
Adkins, Hasil, 164
"Ain't Gonna Do It," 177
"Alice Blue Gown," 135
"(All I Can Do Is) Dream You," 175
All-Time Greatest Hits of Roy Orbison, 174
Alpert, Herb, 91
Alvin, Dave, 177
American Finishing Company, 10
American Recordings, 171
American Studio, 93
Angel, Ronnie, 98
"Another Place, Another Time," 168
Anthony, Rayburn, 135–38
Aristocrat, 7
Armstrong, Louis, xv, 10
Arnold, Eddy, 38, 49
Atkins, Chet, 51, 84
Atlantic, 179
AVI label, 156

Axton, Estelle, 145

B

"Baby, No, No!," 160–61
"Baby Let's Play House," 38, 166
"Baby Ride With Me," 22, 161
Baker, Two-Ton, 96
"Baker Shop Boogie," 160
"Ballad of a Teenage Queen," 80, 81
Baron, Lonnie, 138, 139
Beale Street Shieks, 93, 102, 179
"Bear Cat," 4, 10–11, 160, 163
Bear Family Records, 156, 162, 164, 168, 169, 170, 173, 174, 176
Beatles, The 27, 99
"Be-Bop-A-Lula," 28
Be-Bop Boy, The, 162
Beck, 171
Beeman, B. B., 19
"Beggin' My Baby," 11, 13
"Behind Closed Doors," 151

"Be Mine, All Mine," 138, 177
Benton, Brook, 153
Bernero, Johnny, 70
Berry, Chuck, 29, 76, 99, 172
Best of Sun Rockabilly, The, 177–78
"Big D Jamboree," 38
"Big River," 80, 170
Big Star, 180
Bihari, Joe, viv, 13, 21, 22–23, 117
Bihari, Jules, viv, 13, 21, 22–23, 117
Bihari, Les, 53, 57
Bihari, Saul, viv, 13, 21, 22–23, 117
Bill Black Combo, 59
Bill's Barn, 139
Black, Bill, 27, 31, 104, 108, 166
Black and White Night, A, 175
"Black Cat Bone," 111
Blake, Jim, 113
Blake, Tommy, 178
Bland, Bobby, viv, 3, 9, 14, 19, 150
"Blind Man," 12
Blue Collar Blues, 173

Blue Flames, 161
"Blue Moon," 27, 33–34, 38, 166
Blue Seal Pals, 54
"Blues in the Bottom of My Shoes," 54
"The Blues Is Alright," 12
"Blue Suede Shoes," 115, 160, 169
Blue Velvet, 174
"Blue Waltz," 45
Bobbin label, 11, 13–14
"Bo Diddley," 108
Bond, Eddie, 179
Bono, 174
"Boogie Blues," 45
"The Boogie Disease," 162
"Boogie in the Park," xiii–viv
Boomer's Story, 180
"Booted," 14, 18, 19, 20, 22, 23, 42
"Bottle to the Baby," 55, 165
Bradley, Owen, 88, 89
Bragg, Johnny, 162
Brasfield, Rod, 56
Braxton, George, 139
"Break Up," 149
Brenston, Jackie, viv, 2, 12, 22
Brown, Charles, 18
Brown, J. W., 74
Brown, James, 168
Brown, Myra Gale, 144
Brown, Roy, 26, 166
Brown Derby, 7
Bruce, Edwin, 178
Burgess, Sonny, 29, 36, 78–79, 100, 126, 177
Burlison, Paul, 147, 179
Burnette, Johnny, 28, 179
Burnette Boys, 69
Burns, Panther, 178
Burse, Charlie, 95
Burton, James, 175
Busey, Cary, 49
Bush, Eddie, 131, 136
Butler, Larry, 131–32
Butterfly, 96–97
Byrd, William, 48
Byrds, 176

C

"Cadillac Man," 111, 112, 142, 157, 178–79
Campbell, Little Milton, viv, 2, 3, 11–14, 40–41, 116, 160, 162

"Can't Help Falling in Love," 166
Cantor, Eddie, 6
Cantrell, Bill, 54, 55–57, 58
Carr, James, 59
Cash, Johnny, 38, 41, 45, 71, 74, 78, 79, 80, 81–82, 83, 84, 126, 128, 130, 142, 144, 148, 152, 154, 164, 170–71, 176
Cash, Roy, 79, 80
"'Cause I Love You," 11
Chaffin, Ernie, 164
Charlie Feathers, 165
Charlie Rich, 175
Charlie Rich Sings the Songs of Hank Williams Plus the R&B Sessions, 175
Charly Records, 29, 154, 156, 160–61, 163, 164, 165, 170
Chess, Leonard, viv, 22–23, 162
Chess Records, 4, 11–12, 14, 22, 162–63
"The Chicken," 23, 26
Chilton, Alex, 94, 180
Clark, Casey, 139
Clark, Dick, 79, 100
Classic Cash/Hall of Fame Series, 171
Classic—Jerry Lee Lewis, 167
Classic Johnny Cash, 170
Classics, 169, 173, 176, 177
"Claudette," 174
Claunch, Quinton, 58–59
Clayton, Edgar, 55, 129
Clement, Jack, xv, 60–61, 65–66, 69, 70, 71–72, 73, 78–81, 83–85, 91, 117, 122–23, 142, 152, 171, 174
Clement, Reece, 48, 49, 52, 53–54
Clover Club, 49, 50
Club Handy, 20, 42
Coburn, Kimball, 107, 108
Cochran, Eddie, 28
Cogbill, Tommy, 111
Cohen, Classic, 171
Cole, Nat King, 18, 131
Colin and Kay, 105
"College Man," 177
Colonial Country Club, 102
Columbia, 91, 169
"Come On Down to My House," 95
"Come On Little Mama," 178

Command Performances: The Essential 60's Masters II, 167
Commercial Appeal, 171
Complete 50's Masters, The, 167
Complete Smash Sessions, The, 175
Complete Sun Sessions, The, 165
Connells, 176
Cooder, Ry, 93, 180
Coral, 28
Costello, Elvis, 174
Cotton, James, xi, 2, 162
Cotton Club, 7
"Cotton Crop Blues," xi, 2, 162
Country Ken, 49–50
Counts, Robert, 9
Cowboy Drain, 102
"Crazy About You Baby," 163
"Crazy Arms," 74
Crazy Cavan, 31
Crossthwait, Jimmy, 106–7, 109
Crudup, Arthur, 166
"Cry, Cry, Cry," 170
Cuoghi, Joe, 59
Cuoghi, Ray, 59
"Cute," 107, 108
"Cut Me at 7½," 180

D

Daniel, John, Quartet, 55
Danzig, Glenn, 171
"Darlin," 162
"Daydreamin'," 54, 56
Decca, 169
Deckelman, Bud, 54, 56
"Decorate the Counter," 24, 161, 163
"Defrost Your Heart," 57, 164
Delta Cats, 22
Delta Experimental Projects Compilation Volume 2: Spring Poems, 179
Delta Rhythm Kings, 162
"Devil Doll," 174
Dickerson, Georgia, 9
Dickinson, Cody, 94, 180
Dickinson, Jim, 35–36, 38–39, 85, 92, 93–100, 101–13, 132, 133–35, 157, 178–80
Dickinson, Luther, 94, 180
Dishrag, 96–97
Dixie Flyers, 93–113
"Dixie Fried," 31, 94, 179
Dixieland Drifters, 164
Dixieland Folk-Style, 105

Doctor Ross, 2, 45
"The Dog," 11
"Domino," 174
Domino, Fats, 13
"Don't Be Cruel," 172
"Don't Put No Headstone on
  My Grave," 150, 175
Dora's Nightspot, 24
Dorman, Harold, 89–90
Do the Boogie, 162
"Do the Funky Chicken," 3, 11
"Do the Funky Penguin," 3
*Do the Funky Somethin': The Best
  of Rufus Thomas*, 163
"Do the Push and Pull," 11
Dowdy, Johnny, 8
"Dream Baby," 175
Dreaming My Dreams, 92
Drifters, 139
"Drinkin' Wine," 47, 52–53
Drink Up and Go Home, 164
"Driving Slow," viv
Duke Records, 23, 26, 162–63
Duncan, Billy, 20
Dunn, Duck, 109
Dylan, Bob, 36, 174

E

Earls, Jack, 178
"The Easy Lovin' Plan," 11, 163
Eddy, Duane, 98
Edge, 174
Elk's Club, 7, 8
Ellis, Jimmy, 154
*Elvis: The King of Rock 'n' Roll—
  The Complete 50's Masters*,
  165
Elvis 56, 166
Elvis (a.k.a. Fool), 167
Elvis Classics, 167
Elvis Country, 167
Elvis Now, 167
Elvis Today, 167
Emerson, Billy, 45, 124–25, 160,
  162
"End of the Road," 172
Escott, Colin, 149, 156
*Essential Johnny Cash 1955-83,
  The*, 170
Estes, Sleepy John, 160
"Everybody's Trying to Be My
  Baby," 169

F

Fabulous Charlie Rich, The, 176
Falco, Tav, 94
Fan Club, 179
Feathers, Charlie, 28, 29, 55, 57,
  164, 179
February, 1970: On Stage, 167
"Feelin' Good," 162
"Feel Like Going Home," 151,
  175
Fernwood, 65
Fitzgerald, Bill, 144
Floyd, Harmonica Frank, 45,
  103, 164
"Flying Saucer Rock and Roll,"
  61, 125, 173, 178
Foley, Red, 49
"Folsom Prison Blues," 170
"Forgive Me Lord," 160
"For Sentimental Reasons," 10
Fortune Records, 139
Foster, Fred, 146
Fox and Fortune, 177
Fox Records, 139
Frank, Bob, 102
Franklin, Andy, 167
Freed, Alan, 85–86
Freeman, Charlie, 109, 110
Frizzell, Lefty, 32
*From Nashville to Memphis: The
  Essential 60's Masters I*, 167
Frost, Frank, 145, 163
Fry, John, 111

G

"Gal Named Joe, A," 53
Gardner, Dave, 59
"Get Rhythm," 170
Gillis, George, 106–7
"Girl to Love, A," 42
Gleeves, Cliff, 83
Goat Farm, 7
"Go Go Go," 174
Goldwax, 59
"Gone and Left Me Blues," 179
Gone Gone Gone, 165
"Gonna Dance All Night," 45
*Gonna Have Myself a Ball: The
  Complete 1950s Recordings,*
  164
"Good Rockin' Tonight," xi, 36,
  166
Good Times, 167

Gordon, Rosco, 2, 3, 9, 14, 15,
  23, 35, 42–44, 45, 117, 161,
  162
Gordy, Berry, 144
"Gotta Let You Go," xiii–viv, 157
"Got Your Water Boiling," 89
Grant, Marshall, 80, 170
"Great Balls of Fire," 61, 86, 87,
  119
"Great Medical Menagerist,
  The," 45
Great Original Recordings, The,
  164
Green, Al, 9n
Green, Tuff, 20, 21
"Greenback Dollar," 58
Groove, 150, 175
"Guess Things Happen That
  Way," 80
*Guitar That Changed the World,
  The*, 153
Gunter, Arthur, 166
Gunter, Hardrock, 45
Guralnick, Peter, 115, 167
Guthrie, Woody, 45

H

Hall, Bill, 91
Hall, Horace, 102
Hamblin, Tommy, 63
Hambone's Meditations, 180
Hardin, Neil, 47
Hare, Pat, xi, 2, 20, 161, 162
"Harper Valley P.T.A.," 153
Harris, Courtney, 18
Harris, Ray, 58, 178
Harris, Wynonie, 26
Harrison, George, 174
Harvey, Bill, 23
Hawkins, Martin, 3, 156, 161
Hawkins, Ronnie, 31
Head, Roy, 26
"Her Love Rubbed Off," 169
Herman, Kenneth, 69
"Hey, Boss Man!" 145, 163
"Hey Porter," 170
Hibbert, Toots, 180
Hill, Raymond, 162
Hines, Charles, 98
Hi Records, 136, 150, 175, 176
His First Recordings, 162
*Hittin' That Jug! The Best of
  Sonny Burgess*, 177
Holland, W. S., 128–32, 135–36
Holly, Buddy, 28, 29, 76

Holy Modal Rounders, 106
"Home of the Blues," 50, 170
"Honey Let's Go to the Rock and Roll Show," 139
Hooker, Earl, 2
Hooker, John Lee, 22
Hopkins, Lightnin', 22
Horton, Walter, 2, 9
"Hound Dog," 4, 10, 11
"House Rockin' Boogie," 162
Howlin' Wolf, viv, xi, 1, 2, 3, 22, 23, 96, 99, 134, 160, 161–62
"Howlin' Wolf Boogie," 161
Howlin' Wolf Rides Again, 162
"How Many More Years," 22
Hunter, Ivory Joe, 18

I

"I Can Help," 166
"I Forgot to Remember to Forget," 38, 55
"If Walls Could Talk," 12
"If You Love Me," 14
"I Got a Thing About You Baby," 91
"I'll Be a Good Boy," 3
"I'll Make It All Up to You," 149
"I'll Never Let You Go (Little Darlin')," 38
"I'm a Lonely Man," 11, 14
"I'm Gonna Find Her," 164
"I'm Gonna Murder My Baby," xi, 2, 161, 162
"I'm in the Mood for Love," 10
"I'm Lonesome," 164
"I'm Steady Holdin' On," 11
"In Dreams," 174
Ireland, Ricky, 108
"It's Me, Baby," 47, 53, 164
"It's Now or Never," 123
"I've Been Deceived," 57
"I've Got a Thing About You Baby," 29, 91, 173

J

"Jack, That Cat Was Clean," 174
Jackson, Al, Jr., 93
Jackson, Al, Sr., 93
James, David, 18, 39, 40
Janes, Roland, xv, 44–45, 47, 54, 60–61, 67–72, 73, 74,
76–78, 81–83, 89–91, 100, 104, 125–28, 132–33, 144, 147–48, 150–52, 154–55, 165, 173
Jason and the Scorchers, 94
"Jelly Roll Baker," 10
Jennings, Waylon, 91
Jesters, 134, 157
"Jim Dandy," 111
Johnny Cash at Folsom Prison, 170
Johnny Cash at San Quentin, 170
Johnny Curry's Club, 3
Johnson, Dexter, 55
Johnson, Lonnie, 9–10
Johnson, Robert, 134, 171
Johnson, Terry, 109
Johnson, Willie, 45, 161
Jollyboys Quartet, xiii
Jolson, Al, 6
Jordanaires, 102, 105
"Juice Head Blues," 150
Jungle Fever, 165
"Just a Little Bit," 26
"Just Because," 38
Justis, Bill, 83–85, 92, 93, 102, 103–7, 111–12, 152, 160, 173, 177
"Just Love Me Baby," 26
"Just Rollin' Along," 52
"Just Walking in the Rain," 2, 162

K

Katmandu Quartet, 94, 179
"Kay," 173
Kazak, Ed, 50–51
"Keep What You Got," 162
Keisker, Marion, viv, 51, 52
Kern, Don, 40
Kerr, Anita, Singers, 105
Kesler, Stan, 57, 113, 152, 165
Killer, The, 168
Killer: The Mercury Years, 168
Kilroy, Eddie, 168
King, Albert, 14
King, B. B., viv, 1, 3, 9, 13, 21, 22, 35, 51, 134, 160, 162
King Records, 165
Klein, George, 40, 107
Knight, Jesse, 13
KWEM, 96
Kweskin, Jim, 106
Kyle's Nightclub, 8

L

Lapworth, Sid, 102
Last Train to Memphis: The Rise of Elvis Presley, 167
Ledbetter, Jan, 70
Lee, Dickey, 91
Legendary, The, 174
Leiber, Jerry, 11
"Let Him Try," 42
Let's Bop, 178
"Let the Jukebox Keep On Playing," 58
Lewis, Jerry Lee, viv, xi, 28, 29, 41, 43, 44, 45, 59, 61, 72, 73, 74–75, 76–78, 79, 81, 86, 87, 88, 114, 118–22, 124, 126, 141, 144, 146, 149, 152, 157, 160, 164, 167, 168, 171, 172, 176, 179
Lewis, Sammy, 45
Liberty Records, 176
Like Flies on Sherbert, 180
Lion Music, 11
Little Esther, 20
Littlefield, 103
Little Milton, 40–41
Little Richard, 60, 108
Little Walter Jacobs, 2
Live at the Apollo, 1962, 168
Live at the Star-Club Hamburg, 168
Live in Europe, 168
Locust Years, The, 168
London, Johnny, viv
"The Lonely Bull," 91
"Lonely Weekends," xi, 126, 149–50, 160, 175
Lonely Weekends: The Best of the Sun Years, 175
"Long Black Limousine," 166
"Long Blond Hair," 139, 177
Longhair, Professor, 163
"Look at the Sunshine," 63
"Louie Louie," 175
Louis, Joe Hill, xiii–viv, 2, 22, 157, 160, 162
"Louisiana Hayride," 38
Love, Billy, 18–19, 21
Love, Willie, 12
"Love My Baby," 126, 178
"Loverboy," 84
"Love You 'Til the Day I Die," 14, 19
Lynch, David, 174
Lynne, Jeff, 174

M

Mallett, Ray, 140
"Man in Love," 164
Manker, Sid, 103–4
Mann, Carl, 128, 129, 130–31, 135, 148–49
Man Son, 20
"Marie," 21
"The Marine Band Hymn," 167
Mar-Keys, 98
Martin, Edwin, 4
Martin, Jimmy, 131
Martindale, Wink, 107
Mashburn, Gordon, 49, 52
Matthews, Red, 59
Maynard, Marvin, 138–39
McCracklin, Jimmy, 26
McGee, Stick, 47
McQueen, J. P. "Doc," 69
McVoy, Carl, 59
"Me and My Rhythm Guitar," 142
Memphis Days: The Definitive Edition, 161
Memphis Jug Band, 95
Memphis Masters, The Best of B. B. King, The, 162
Memphis Ramble, 164
Memphis Recording Service, xiii, 1, 2, 4, 22, 145
Mercury Records, 168, 175
Meteor Records, 11, 13, 28, 53, 57
"Midnight in Moscow," 105
"Midnite Blues," 150
"Milkcow Blues Boogie," 36
Million Dollar Quartet, The, 171, 172
Minga, Tommy, 110
Mitchell, Sunbeam, 20
"Moanin' at Midnight," 161
Modern Records, viv
"Mohair Sam," 164
Moman, Chips, 69, 91, 111
"Mona Lisa," 130–31, 136
"Monkey Man," 94, 109, 179
Monroe, Bill, 27, 34
Monument, 174, 179
Moody Blue, 167
Moore, Bob, 84
Moore, Don, 140
Moore, Scotty, 27, 29, 31–34, 107–9, 144, 145–47, 148–50, 152–53, 166

Moore, Tommy, 139, 140
Morrow, James, 174
"The Most Beautiful Girl," 151
Motown Records, 142
"Mountain of Love," 89–90
"Mr. Highway Man," 161
Mud Boy, 94, 179
Muddy Waters, 2, 99
"My Babe," 111, 112, 134, 178
"My Baby She's Gone," 139
"My Baby Walked Off," xi, 161
"My Heart Cries Out for You," 175
Mystery Girl, 174
"Mystery Train," 2, 36, 38, 162, 166, 178

N

Nelson, Clarence, 111
Neutrons, 94, 179
"Night Train from Chicago," 111
Nix, Don, 109
Nix, Willie, 160
"No More Doggin'," 19–20, 21, 163
"No Name Girl," 173
"No She Cares No More for Me," 45
"Not Alone Any More," 174

O

O. J. Records, 59
"Oh My Darlin'," 63
O'Neal, Johnny, 162
"One Hand Loose," 55, 165
"One Has My Heart," 168
O'Neil, Pat, 73
"One More Time," 89
"The One Rose," 48
"Only the Lonely," 175
"Ooby Dooby," 173
Orbison, Roy, viv, xv, 28, 78, 148, 154, 162, 173–75, 176
Otis, Johnny, 20

P

Paige, Teddy, 110–11
Palace Theater, 7

Paragons, 139
Parker, Junior, viv, 1, 2, 3, 41, 162, 178
Parker, Tom, 38
Park Lane, 95
"Patches," 91
Patton, Charley, 1
Pavlick, Johnny, 137–38
Peacock Records, 11
Peck, Cliff, 47
Pepper, Marvin, 73–74
Perkins, Carl, viv, 29, 31, 38, 55, 57, 63, 72, 115, 118, 126, 128, 136, 140, 141, 142, 144, 148, 157, 164, 169, 171, 172, 176
Perkins, Luther, 80, 81–82, 170
Peterson, Earl, 45
Petty, Tom, 174
Phillips, Dewey, xiii, 35, 43, 52–53, 99, 100, 112, 180–81
Phillips, Jerry, 110
Phillips, Jud, xiii, 38, 79
Phillips, Knox, 110, 134
Phillips, Sam, xi, xiii, 1–3, 4, 14, 18, 23, 26, 27, 28, 29, 31, 32–35, 36, 41, 42, 43, 44, 50, 53, 54, 58, 69, 72–73, 78, 79, 82, 83, 84–85, 87–89, 94, 103, 109, 111–12, 114–21, 135, 136, 137, 140, 142–44, 145, 149, 152–53, 154–55, 156, 162, 163, 175
Phillips International, 126
Pictures and Paintings, 151, 176
Pittman, Barbara, 58, 59
Play Me Records, 92
Pleased to Meet Me, 180
"Please Throw This Old Dog a Bone," 17
Poindexter, Doug, 32, 45
Pop and the Midnight Ramblers, 67
Powers, Johnny, 138–42, 177
Presley, Elvis, viv, xi, 1, 2, 14, 27, 29, 31, 33, 34, 35, 36, 38, 39–40, 41, 42, 45, 52, 57, 59, 60, 77, 91, 99, 114, 123, 130, 134, 141, 144, 152, 154, 157, 162, 165, 166, 169, 171, 172, 175, 176
Presley, Priscilla, 123
Pride, Charley, 92
Prisonaires, 2, 160
"Problem Child," 174
Promised Land, 167
Purcell, Bill, 102

R

Rabbit Foot Minstrels, 7, 8
Rainey, Ma, 160
Randolph, Boots, 102
Rare Tracks, 168
"Raunchy," 103, 126, 152, 160, 177
Rauzy, Bill, 107
RCA, 38, 160, 171
Rebel Rockability, 177
"Rebound," 150
"Red Cadillac and a Black Mustache," 176
Redding, Otis, 168
"Red Headed Woman," 177
"Red Hot," 86, 99, 124, 125, 173, 178, 179
Red Hot: The Best of Billy Lee Riley, 173
Red Hot and Blue, 180
"Red Hot and Blue" show, 35, 53, 180
Reed, Jimmy, 98
The Regents, 97
REM, 176
Replacements, 94
Reverend Horton Heat, 141
Rhino Records, 161, 164, 168, 170, 179
Rhodes, Slim, 55, 164
Rich, Charlie, viv, xi, xv, 43, 141, 144, 149–50, 151–52, 154, 160, 173, 175–76
Richberg, John, 112
Riles, Jake, 49
Riley, Billy Lee, 29, 36, 44, 60–65, 69, 72–75, 78–79, 85–91, 99, 112, 117–26, 172–73, 176, 178, 179
Riley, Jeannie C., 153
Ripley Cotton Choppers, 45, 51
Robey, Don, 11, 23
Rockabilly Stars, 151
Rock-A-Billy Records, 179
Rock and Roll Trio and Their Rockin' Friends from Memphis, 179
Rock Baby, 178
"Rock Boppin' Baby," 178
"Rocket 88," viv, 2, 12, 22, 160
"Rockhouse," 79, 174
Rockin' 6os, The, 178
"Rockin' Chair Daddy," 157
"Rockin' on the Moon," 88
"Rockin' With My Baby," 53, 54
Rock It, 178

"Rock 'n' Roll Ruby," 176
"Rock Rock," 139
"Rock With Me Baby," 70
Rocky-A-Billy, 164
Rodgers, Jimmie, 62
Rolling Stones, 36, 99
"Romp and Stomp," 164
"Rooster Blues," 179
Roots of Rock, The, 177
Rosco's Rhythm, 163
Ross, Isiah, 162
Rossini, Tony, 144
Rounder Records, 161, 162, 177, 178
"Rowboat," 171
RPM Records, viv, 14, 22, 162–63
Rubin, Rick, 171
Rufus, Thomas, 39–40
Ryles, John Wesley, 173

S

"Saddled the Cow (And Milked the Horse)," 14
Sain, Oliver, 14
"St. Louis Blues," 135, 136
Sales, Mac, 53
Sam Phillips Recording, 44
Sanders, Arnold, 48
Sanders, Richard, 20
"Save That Money," 11
Scaife, Cecil, 144
Scott, Jack, 139
Selvidge, Sid, 102
"Send Me Some Lovin'," 108
Serrat, Howard, 45
Set Me Free, 176
Shade, Will, 95, 106
"Shake 'em On Down," 179
Shakin' Black, 179
Sherrill, Billy, 146, 151, 153
"She Thinks I Still Care," 91
"Shimmy Shimmy Walk," 173
"Shoobie Oobie," 20
Silver Linings, 176
Sims, Willie, 13
"The Singing Salesman," 48
Singleton, Shelby, xv, 91, 153, 154, 167, 173
Sire Records, 176
Sister Lovers, 94
"Sittin' and Thinkin'," 150
Skaggs, Ricky, 81
Skynyrd, Lynyrd, 169
Smith, Warren, 107, 108, 144, 152, 176, 177
Smokey Joe, 164

"Smokie, Part 2," 59
Snow, Hank, 38
"So Long, I'm Gone," 176
Some Think He Might Be Kind, 154
Sonny Burgess, 177
Southern Jubilee's, 160
Southtown Records, 94, 179
Spector, Phil, 144
"Spinout," 166, 167
"Split Personality," 164
Springsteen, Bruce, 175
Stamps, Al, 98
Starlight Wranglers, 32
Star Rhythm Boys, 49, 50
Star Talent, 3, 4
Stax Studio, 39, 91, 93
Steel, Gene, 48
Steel, Willie, 161
"Steel Guitar Rag," 50
Stevenson, Wee Willie, 131, 136, 137
Stewart, Jim, 145
Stoller, Mike, 11
Stompin', 163
Stoots, Ronnie, 108
"Strange Things Happening," 99, 180
Stray Cats, 31
Sugar Ditch Records, 180
Suggs, Brad, 138
Summer Records, 91
Sun Blues Archive series, 161
Sun Blues Years, The, 160, 161, 163
Sun Box, The, 160
Sun Country Years, The, 163
Sun International, 91, 154, 173
Sun Records, xiv–xv, 4, 11, 12, 13, 23, 27, 28, 45, 57, 60, 65–66, 78, 81, 93, 99, 112–13, 114–15, 126, 130, 131, 137, 139, 142, 153, 156
Sun Records Collection, The, 157, 160
Sun Records Harmonica Classics, 161
Sun Records—The Rockin' Years, 177
Sun Rockabilly: The Classic Recordings, 178
Sun's Greatest Hits, 178
Sun Years, The, 162, 170, 174
"Sure to Fall," 58
"Suspicious Minds," 166
"Swamp Root," 45
Swan, Billy, 31
"Sweet and Easy to Love," 79
"Sweet Home Alabama," 169
"Sweet Sixteen," 111

T

Talley, Robert, 39
Tate, C. W., 13
Taylor, Bill, 45, 164
"Tear It Up," 28
"Tell Me Why You Like Roosevelt," 99
Tennessee Border, 177
"Ten Years," 84
"Thanks a Lot," 149
Tharpe, Sister Rosetta, 99, 180
That Rockabilly Cat!, 165
"That's All Right," 33, 34, 42–43, 157, 166
That's the Way It Is, 167
"There Won't Be Anymore," 150
They Walk Among Us, 179
"Think Before You Go," 70
Third/Sister Lovers, 180
Thomas, B. J., 123
Thomas, Carla, 10, 11, 39
Thomas, Mavis, 10
Thomas, Raymond, 17
Thomas, Rufus, viv, 2, 3–11, 14, 17, 35, 41, 43, 51, 163
Thompson, Hayden, 126, 178
Thornton, Big Mama, 4
Thornton, Willie Mae, 10
"Three O'Clock Blues," 21
Tidwell, George, 104
"Tiger Man," 11
Tip Top Daddy, 165
Tobin, Idella, 15
Tolley, Frank, 50, 53
"Tongue-Tied Jill," 165
Toots Hibbert, 94
Toots in Memphis, 180
Townshend, Raspers, 48
"Tragedy," 107, 145
"Train Kept A-Rollin'," 28
"Train of Love," 170
Traveling Wilburys Volume One, The, 174
"Treat Her Right," 26
"Trouble Bound," 70
"Troublesome Waters," 45
True Believers, 94
"Trumpet," 47
"Trying to Get to You," 38, 173
Tubb, Ernest, 46–47, 80
Turner, Bonnie, 22, 162
Turner, Ike, 12–14, 21, 22, 41, 116, 162
Turner, Joe, 26
Turner, Tina, 22

U

"Ubangi Stomp," 144
Uh Huh Honey, 165
Unchained, 171
Underwood, Charles, 144, 152
"The Unicorn," 106
Up Through the Years, 168, 169, 170

V

Van Eaton, J. M., 54, 60, 71–72, 73, 91, 126, 138, 141, 149, 150, 165, 173
Vaughan, Ira Lynn, 89
Vaughn, Ben, 165
Vee-Jay Records, 26
Velvet Underground, 176
Vincent, Gene, 28, 169
Vinson, Mose, 160
"Vision to Version," 42
"Voice of a Fool," 59

W

Wainwright, Loudon, 171
Waits, Tom, 171
Walcott, Frank S., 8
Walk a Mile in My Shoes: The Essential 70's Masters, 167
Walker, Mel, 20
"Walking the Dog," 3, 11, 163
"Walkin' in the Rain," 160
Wallace, Slim, 65, 70
Washington, Dinah, 153
Water from the Wells of Home, 171
"Way Down in the Congo," 162
Wayne, Thomas, 107, 145, 146
"Ways of a Woman in Love, The," 80, 149
WDIA, 3, 10, 14, 17, 18, 39, 40, 96
"Wedding Gown of White," 57
"We're Gonna Make It," 12
"We Wanna Boogie," 177
Wexler, Jerry, 103
"What's Made Milwaukee Famous (Has Made a Loser Out of Me)," 168
Whiskey Chute, 95
White, Tony Joe, 173

"Whole Lotta Shakin' Goin' On," xi, 157, 160
"Whose Gonna Shoe Your Pretty Feet," 135
"Who Will the Next Fool Be," 150
"Wild Horses," 93
Wilkes, Mary, 21
Wilkes, Willie, 21. 20
Wilkins, Joe Willie, 12, 20
Williams, Don, 92
Williams, Hank, 72, 99, 164
Williams, Jimmy, 139
Williams, Nat D., 3, 5, 6–7, 17, 35
Williams, Sonny Boy, 12
Willis, Chuck, 13
Willis, Martin, 74, 90, 138, 149, 150
Wills, Bob, 28
Wilson, Jackie, 172
Wilson, Jimmy, 71, 74
Wilson, Kimmons, 153
Windbreakers, 176
Winn, Miles Red, 48
"With Your Love, With Your Kiss," 138
WJOI, 55
WMC, 46
WMPS, 65
Wood, Anita, 107
"Worried About My Baby," 162
Wray, Link, 98
WSM, 56

Y

"Yakety Yak," 52, 53
Yelvington, Malcolm, 28, 45, 47, 50, 51, 128, 164
"You Don't Know Me," 166
"You'll Do It All the Time," 93, 102, 113, 179
"You're a Heartbreaker," 38
"Your Love," 139
"Your True Love," 130, 169

Z

Zee, Don, 139
Zu-Zazz, 164, 175

JOHN FLOYD has spent most of his life in Memphis, Tennessee, and worked there from 1991 to 1994 as the music editor of the *Memphis Flyer*. His essays, profiles, and reviews have appeared in numerous publications, including *Musician, Option, Rock & Rap Confidential*, and the *Journal of Country Music*. Floyd was an editor and contributor to the *All Music Guide* and the music editor of the *Miami New Times*.

DAVE MARSH was a founding editor of *Creem* and an editor at *Rolling Stone*, where he created *The Rolling Stone Record Guide*. He is now a music critic at *Playboy*, publisher of *Rock & Rap Confidential*, and a prolific author of books about music and popular culture, including books about Elvis Presley, Michael Jackson, and the song "Louie Louie." His book *Before I Get Old* is the definitive biography of the Who, and *Glory Days* and *Born to Run*, both about Bruce Springsteen, were best-sellers.